SHEPARD

in an hour

BY LAURA J. GRAHAM

SUSAN C. MOORE, SERIES EDITOR

PLAYWRIGHTS in an hour
know the playwright, love the play
IN AN HOUR BOOKS • HANOVER, NEW HAMPSHIRE • INANHOURBOOKS.COM
AN IMPRINT OF SMITH AND KRAUS PUBLISHERS, INC • SMITHANDKRAUS.COM

With grateful thanks to Carl R. Mueller, whose fascinating introductions to his translations of the Greek and German playwrights provided inspiration for this series.

Published by In an Hour Books
an imprint of Smith and Kraus, Inc.
177 Lyme Road, Hanover, NH 03755
inanhourbooks.com SmithandKraus.com

Know the playwright, love the play.

Manufactured in the United States of America
First edition: April 2010
10 9 8 7 6 5 4 3 2 1

Front cover design by Dan Mehling, dmehling@gmail.com
Text design by Kate Mueller, Electric Dragon Productions
Book production by Dede Cummings Design, DCDesign@sover.net

ISBN-13: 978-1-936232-25-3
ISBN-10: 1-936232-25-1
Library of Congress Control Number: 2009943234

CONTENTS

Why Playwrights in an Hour?

This new series by Smith and Kraus Publishers titled Playwrights in an Hour has a dual purpose for being: one academic, the other general. For the general reader, this volume, as well as the many others in the series, offers in compact form the information needed for a basic understanding and appreciation of the works of each volume's featured playwright. Which is not to say that there don't exist volumes on end devoted to each playwright under consideration. But inasmuch as few are blessed with enough time to read the splendid scholarship that is available, a brief, highly focused accounting of the playwright's life and work is in order. The central feature of the series, a thirty- to forty-page essay, integrates the playwright into the context of his or her time and place. The volumes, though written to high standards of academic integrity, are accessible in style and approach to the general reader as well as to the student and, of course, to the theater professional and theatergoer. These books will serve for the brushing up of one's knowledge of a playwright's career, to the benefit of theater work or theatergoing. The Playwrights in an Hour series represents all periods of Western theater: Aeschylus to Shakespeare to Wedekind to Ibsen to Williams to Beckett, and on to the great contemporary playwrights who continue to offer joy and enlightenment to a grateful world.

Carl R. Mueller
School of Theater, Film and Television
Department of Theater
University of California, Los Angeles

Introduction

Sam Shepard's unpredictable career falls into at least two periods, possibly three. The first features the East Village space cadet of *La Turista*, *The Unseen Hand*, and *Cowboy Mouth*, when Shepard seems to be dreaming poetic phantasmagorias through a haze of narcotics. At this time, Shepard — a companion to his collaborator on *Cowboy Mouth,* Patti Smith, and a drummer for the Holy Modal Rounders — is bouncing his plays against an aural background of hard-rock music and the nasally twang of Southern California. Perhaps the best-known play of this period, *The Tooth of Crime*, actually features a combat between an older and a younger musician for primacy in the world of rock.

Hallucination, frenzied music, and the battle between old age and youth, these are the hallmarks of Shephard's generally short plays that brought him a growing reputation and a limited Off-Off-Broadway audience. During a trip to London in the early 1970s, however, when Shepard was exposed to the explosive eloquence of the Royal Court Theatre movement and met such masters of the form as Harold Pinter and director Peter Brook, his art underwent a significant sea change. This led to what he once described to me as his "English period," where the typical Shepard dreamscape is forced into the background, lurking behind an essentially realistic and domestic mise-en-scene.

One of the earliest plays in this genre is *Curse of the Starving Class*, its title a mischievous gloss on the old adage that "drink was the curse of the working class." Set in a rundown kitchen, complete with refrigerator and stove, the play seemed to suggest that Shepard was abandoning his Expressionist legacy and joining Arthur Miller, Tennessee Williams, and Edward Albee in the world of American family drama. So did another play of that period, *Buried Child*, which, located in the Midwest rather than California, is an almost Ibsenite allegory about how the hidden sins of a family are eventually exposed to view, like vegetables pushing through the fallow earth. The play's final image of Tilden coming onstage with a dead baby in his arms encased in husks of corn is one of the most powerful in all of modern drama.

It was during this English period that Shepard found fame as a Hollywood actor and was nominated for an Academy Award for his performance as Chuck Yeager in *The Right Stuff.* Having repaired a broken front tooth, married a movie star (Jessica Lange), and built a stable of horses, Shepard seemed to be falling victim to the Curse of the Celebrity Class. He even began to play polo, like Tom Buchanan in Fitzgerald's *The Great Gatsby,* and constructed a swimming pool, like Gatsby himself (also like Gatsby, he probably never used it). But unlike Fitzgerald's hero, Shepard was hardly trying to live out his Platonic image of himself. Quite the contrary, it was toward the end of this period that Shepard began his most serious and dangerous work, first as a critic of the Protestant ethic and family and marital relationships in such plays as *True West* and a *Fool for Love,* and then later as a critic of America's growing belligerent posture and unchecked ability to suspend civil rights.

Perhaps because of his occasional collaborations with director Joseph Chaikin of the activist Open Theatre, Shepard was beginning to display a new, or perhaps newly reinforced, political conscience in such plays as *States of Shock*, *Simpatico*, and *The God of Hell.* In that last work particularly, Shepard offers what may very well be the fiercest and most radical critique to date of the government rationale for the Iraq war, American torture procedures, and invasions of privacy.

Thus, Shepard has exchanged a radical formal trademark for a radical social-political agenda, following the same path as Henrik Ibsen who suppressed the powerful poetic instincts he displayed in such earlier plays as *Brand* and *Peer Gynt* in order to document the sins of modern life in such plays as *Ghosts* and *The Wild Duck.* In Ibsen's case, this was the act of a genuine saint of the theater. In the case of Sam Shepard, it is the choice of an artist who never ceases to grow, to explore, to confront, and to listen to new music.

Robert Brustein
Founding Director of the Yale and American Repertory Theatres
Distinguished Scholar in Residence, Suffolk University
Senior Research Fellow, Harvard University

Shepard

IN A MINUTE

AGE	DATE	
—	**1943**	**Enter Sam Shepard, born Samuel Shepard Rogers VII.**
2	1945	New York Yankee baseball club sold for $3 million.
3	1946	"Zip-a-dee-doo-dah," from Disney's *Song of the South,* is a hit.
4	1947	*The Diary of Anne Frank* is published.
5	1948	"Citation" wins KentuckyDerby, Belmont, and Preakness Stakes with Eddie Arcaro riding.
7	1950	North Korea invades South Korea.
8	1951	J. D. Salinger —*The Catcher in the Rye*
14	1957	Jack Kerouac — *On the Road*
15	1958	Harold Pinter — *The Birthday Party*
17	1960	Protesting segregation, black students sit at whites-only lunch counters in Greensboro, N.C.
20	1963	Russian astronaut Valentina Tereshkova is the first woman in space.
21	**1964**	**Sam Shepard — *Cowboys***
24	1967	Tom Stoppard —*Rosencrantz and Guildenstern Are Dead*
25	1968	Jordanian Sirhan Sirhan assassinates Senator Robert F. Kennedy in LA.
27	**1970**	**Sam Shepard — *Operation Sidewinder***
31	1974	Inflation and the price of oil soar, causing gas shortages in the U.S.
33	**1976**	**Sam Shepard — *Suicide in B-Flat***
35	1978	National Lampoon's *Animal House* defies standards of decency.
36	1979	U.S. and Communist China establish full diplomatic relations.
37	**1980**	**Sam Shepard — *True West***
40	1983	Michael Jackson's "Thriller" sets all time high for record sales.
41	1984	Donald Duck celebrates his fiftieth birthday.
46	1989	Iran's Ayatollah Khomeini issues a fatwa against Salman Rushdie.
50	1993	The Catholic Church forbids artificial birth control.
51	**1994**	**Sam Shepard — *Simpatico***
55	1998	President Bill Clinton faces impeachment before Congress.
56	1999	After a forty-nine-year career, the "Peanuts" comic strip ends its run.
61	**2004**	**Sam Shepard —*The God of Hell***
63	2006	Google acquires YouTube for $1.65 billion.
66	**2009**	**Sam Shepard — *Ages of the Moon***

A snapshot of the playwright's world. From historical events to pop-culture and the literary landscape of the time, this brief list catalogues events that directly or indirectly impacted the playwright's writing. Play citations refer to premiere dates.

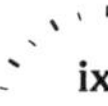

HIS WORKS

DRAMATIC WORKS

Cowboys
Rock Garden
Up to Thursday
Dog
Rocking Chair
Chicago
Icarus's Mother
4-H Club
Fourteen Hundred Thousand
Red Cross
Cowboys #2
La Turista
Melodrama Play
Forensic and the Navigators
The Holy Ghostly
The Unseen Hand
Operation Sindwinder
Shaved Splits
Mad Dog Blues
Cowboy Mouth
Back Bog Beast Bait
The Tooth of the Crime
Geography of a Horse Dreamer
Little Ocean
Action and *Killer's Head*
Angel City

This section presents a complete list of the playwright's works in chronological order.

Suicide in Bb
Inacoma
The Sad Lament of Pecos Bill on the Eve of Killing His Wife
Tongues (co-written with Joseph Chaikin)
Curse of the Starving Class
Buried Child
Savage/Love (co-written with Joseph Chaikin)
Seduced
True West
Fool for Love
A Lie of the Mind
True Dylan
States of Shock
Simpatico
When the World Was Green (A Chef's Fable) (co-written with Joseph Chaikin)
Eyes for Consuela
The Late Henry Moss
The God of Hell
Kicking a Dead Horse
Ages of the Moon

PROSE, POETRY, AND SHORT STORIES

Hawk Moon
Rolling Thunder Logbook
Motel Chronicles
Cruising Paradise
Great Dream of Heaven

SCREENPLAYS

Me and My Brother (co-written with Robert Frank)
Zabriskie Point (co-written with Michelangelo Antonioni, Fred Gardner, Tonino Guerra and Clare Peploe)
Maxagasm: A Distorted Western for Soul & Psyche (unproduced)
Bodyguard (unproduced)

Ringaleevio (co-written with Murray Mednick, unproduced)
Oh! Calcutta! (writing contributor)
Renaldo and Clara (co-written with Bob Dylan)
Paris, Texas
Fool for Love
Far North
Silent Tongue
Curse of the Starving Class (writer of play, screenplay by Bruce Beresford)
Simpatico, (writer of play, screenplay by David Nichols IV and Matthew Warchus)
Don't Come Knocking (co-written with Wem Wenders)

TV SCRIPTS

True West

RADIO SCRIPTS

Blue Bitch
The War in Heaven: Angel's Monologue (co-written with Joseph Chaikin)

FILM APPEARANCES

Renaldo and Clara
Days of Heaven
Resurrection
Raggedy Man
Frances
The Right Stuff
Country
Fool for Love
Crimes of the Heart
Baby Boom
Steel Magnolias
The Voyager
Defenseless
Thunderheart

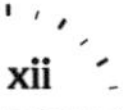

The Pelican Brief
Dash and Lily
Snow Falling on Cedars
Purgatory
Hamlet
All the Pretty Horses
Black Hawk Down
Kurosawa
Shot in the Heart
Swordfish
The Pledge
The Notebook
Don't Come Knocking
Bandidas
Stealth
Walker Payne
The Return
Charlotte's Web (narrator)
Ruffian
The Assassination of Jesse James by the Coward Robert Ford
The Accidental Husband
Felon

Onstage with Shepard

Introducing Colleagues and Contemporaries of Sam Shepard

THEATER

Edward Albee, American playwright
David Hare, English playwright
Beth Henley, American playwright
David Rabe, American playwright
Wole Soyinka, Nigerian playwright
Luis Valdez, American playwright
Wendy Wasserstein, American playwright
August Wilson, American playwright

ARTS

Merce Cunningham, American dancer
Bob Dylan, American musician
Mick Jagger, English musician
John Lennon, English musician
Lou Reed, American musician
Keith Richards, English musician
Mark Rothko, Latvian-American painter
Galina Ulanova, Russian ballerina
Andy Warhol, American pop artist

FILM

Woody Allen, American filmmaker
Richard Burton, Welsh actor
Judi Dench, English actress
James Earl Jones, American actor

This section lists contemporaries whom the playwright may or may not have known.

Jesssica Lange, American actress
Spike Lee, American filmmaker
Sidney Poitier, American actor
Martin Scorsese, American actor

POLITICS/ MILITARY

Osama bin Laden, Saudi Arabian militant Islamic terrorist
Bill Clinton, American president
Queen Elizabeth II, English head of state
Mikhail Gorbachev, Soviet president
Nelson Mandela, South African activist and president
François Mitterrand, French president
Ronald Reagan, American president
Margaret Thatcher, British prime minister

SCIENCE

Francis Crick, Englsih biogist, physicist, and neuroscientist
William DeVries, American surgeon
Paul Farmer, American anthropologist and physician
Enrico Fermi, Italian physicist
Dian Fossey, American zoologist
Jane Goodall, English biologist
Stephen Hawking, English physicist
John Forbes Nash, American mathematician and economist

LITERATURE

Isabel Allende, Chilean author
Truman Capote, American writer
Michael Crichton, American novelist
Erica Jong, American novelist
Jack Kerouac, American novelist and poet
Salman Rushdie, Indian-British novelist
Kurt Vonnegut Jr., American novelist
Tom Wolfe, American novelist

RELIGION/ PHILOSOPHY

Noam Chomsky, American philosopher
Dalai Lama, Tibetan political and religious leader
Ruhollah Khomeini, Iranian religious leader and politician
Martin Luther King Jr., American civil rights activist
Mother Teresa, Albanian Catholic nun
Pope Jean Paul II, Polish leader of the Catholic Church
Rick Warren, American Evangelical minister
Rowan Williams, Welsh Archbishop of Canterbury

SPORTS

Muhammad Ali, American boxer
Arthur Ashe, American tennis player
Bjôrn Borg, Swedish tennis player
Jim Brown, American football player
Earvin "Magic" Johnson Jr., American basketball player
Willie Mays, American baseball player
Arnold Palmer, American golfer

INDUSTRY/ BUSINESS

Richard Branson, English industrialist
Warren Buffett, American businessman
Larry Ellison, American businessman
Allan Greenspan, American Federal Reserve chairman
Steve Jobs, American cofounder of Apple, Inc.
Ingvar Kamprad, Swedish founder of Ikea
Carlos Slim, Mexican businessman
Muhammad Yunus, Bangladeshi economist and banker

SHEPARD

Sam Shepard, one of America's greatest living playwrights, has exerted a profound influence on the contemporary stage. His plays are widely performed on Broadway and off, in all the major regional American theaters, and throughout Europe. In 1979, he received the Pulitzer Prize for Drama for his play *Buried Child*, which established his national reputation. Of his more than forty-five plays, eleven of them have won Obie Awards.

Shepard is also an accomplished actor, television and film director, screenwriter, and musician. In addition, he is the author of several books of short stories, essays, and memoirs. His screenplay for *Paris, Texas* won the Golden Palm Award at the 1984 Cannes Film Festival. Among his roles as an actor, Shepard portrayed pilot Chuck Yeager in *The Right Stuff* (1983), for which he was nominated for an Academy Award for Best Supporting Actor.

GROWING UP

Sam Shepard was born Samuel Shepard Rogers VII to Samuel Rogers VI and Jane Elaine Schook Rogers, at the army outpost of Fort

---

This is the core of the book. The essay places the playwright in the context of his or her world and analyzes the influences and inspirations within that world.

Sheridan, Illinois, on November 5, 1943. In the year of Shepard's birth, America and the Allies were deeply embroiled in World War II. During that worldwide conflict, the United States would emerge as a leader, a position that would continue well past the end of the war.

Shepard's father was a member of the Army Air Corps and a bomber pilot in World War II. Shepard remembers a transitory early childhood, as the family moved from army base to army base before his father retired from the service in 1949. His father's military service had a profound influence on Shepard. His apparent admiration for the service and his understanding of how this military experience helped to shape the distant man that his father became is notable in several of his plays and prose pieces.

World War II would radically change the economy and social environment of the United States. The postwar years saw a remarkable period of economic growth and prosperity accompanied by the baby boom. Encouraged by the GI Bill — the Servicemen's Readjustment Act of 1944 that provided loans to returning servicemen — an unprecedented number of veterans bought houses and started families. Many of the young troops did not return to their hometowns but settled in new areas across the country and even Hawaii where many had been stationed. The once largely rural nation was transformed to a largely urban and suburban one — a transformation that Shepard addressed in many of his plays, particularly *Curse of the Starving Class* (1978) and *Buried Child* (1978).

Shepard's father was born in 1917 in Crystal Lake, a small town outside Chicago, where his ancestors had long and strong roots. When he returned from the war with shrapnel wounds, he chose not to return to that community. Neither did the family continue their transient lifestyle of living on various army bases. Instead, Sam VI settled his family in 1955 in the largely middle-class California suburb of South Pasadena.

Later, in 1955, when Shepard was twelve, the family moved to a working avocado ranch with horses, chickens, and sheep in Duarte,

California. Duarte was a decidedly stratified community made up of the wealthy, middle class, and poor, with a sizeable Mexican-American population. Shepard tried to help run the increasingly ramshackle ranch but was hampered by escalating familial conflicts. His hard-drinking father frequently disappeared from the ranch, When he was present, violent arguments between father and son increased. Between his dysfunctional family relationships and economic hardship, Shepard came to identify himself as an outsider in the community, someone from the "wrong side of the tracks," according to Don Shewey in *Sam Shepard.*

Working the ranch, Shepard developed a lifelong attachment to the land and animals, especially horses. In his teens, he worked as a stable hand on the Conley Arabian Horse Ranch in Chino. He later became an enthusiastic polo player and owns horses currently. After graduating from Duarte High in 1960, Shepard spent a year at Mount Saint Antonio Junior College, majoring in agricultural science. He began to dream of escape, however, from his troubled family and conflicted relationship with his father.

ESCAPE TO NEW YORK CITY

After acting in a few college plays, Shepard auditioned to join the touring Bishop's Company Repertory Players and, when accepted, took the opportunity to escape his small community and dysfunctional family. He toured the country in 1962 but left the troupe to remain in New York City in 1963.

Shepard had been nicknamed Steve, a family tradition meant to distinguish him from his father. After moving to New York, he changed his name from Steve Rogers to Sam Shepard — a decision that underscores Shepard's focus on the individual's need to create an identity distinct from that inherited from the family.

Shepard worked at various jobs in New York City, including a stint as a security guard, before reuniting with high-school friend Charles Mingus Jr., son of the great jazz musician. With Mingus' help,

Shepard got a job bussing tables at the popular nightclub the Village Gate, where he saw and heard some of the best comedians, singers, and jazzmen of the day. There he also met Ralph Cook, founder of Theatre Genesis.

The small theaters were hungry for new plays, and Cook urged Shepard to write plays. *Cowboys* and *The Rock Garden*, Shepard's first one-acts, were soon performed on a double bill as the second production mounted by Theatre Genesis at St. Mark's Church in October 1964. Shepard wrote further one-acts quickly, many of them produced in Off-Off-Broadway venues, and he rapidly developed an enthusiastic following in that theatrical community.

When Shepard began his playwrighting career in New York City in the 1960s, the Off-Off-Broadway movement was just emerging. At that time, theater producers were faced with competition from the new medium of television, which led to the increased commercialism of Broadway and even of the Off-Broadway movement. The Off-Off-Broadway movement was a reaction against this commercialism and against the traditions of realistic theater. The theatrical styles of Realism and Naturalism, dominant in American and European theater from the late 1800s to the late 1950s and early 1960s and encapsulated in the plays of Eugene O'Neill and Tennessee Williams, gave way to young playwrights who were experimenting in nonrealistic styles. The year 1968, in particular, marked a dramatic turning point in American theater. In that year, the production of *Hair!* introduced nudity and obscenity to the stage. The following year, *Che!* brought explicit sexual acts onstage, and many of the scenes in *Oh, Calcutta!*, which included a monologue from Shepard's *The Rock Garden*, were performed entirely in the nude.

All this theatrical experimentation resulted in the establishment of small theaters such as The Caffe Cino, the Judson Poets' Theatre, Café La Mama, and Theatre Genesis. These theaters were dedicated to encouraging unknown playwrights and avant-garde theatrical techniques. The young writers and directors involved shared a theatrical vision grounded not in the traditions of dramatic literature but in the new "pop mythology" — informed by film, commercials, television, comic strips, the drug culture, and contemporary music. They experimented with techniques of Expressionism, Impressionism, and Surrealism. Their objective was to present the subjective, internal reality of their characters rather than the familiar, naturalistically drawn characters of Realism.

Early on, Shepard became known by his peers, audiences, and critics alike as one of the most compelling of the new playwrights. His style was unique, especially in the urban East, as his plays explored the myths of the cowboy and the American West. He contrasted a healthy Native American culture with a dysfunctional and conflicted contemporary America. Technological developments achieved during and just after World War II had "put America on the road," ushering in the idea of freedom and possible prosperity brought about by mobility. Disappointment in the "myth of mobility," in mass consumption, built-in product obsolescence, and the disintegration of individual independence as well as the nuclear family informs Shepard's entire canon. In the early play*The Unseen Hand* (1969), the mythic figure Blue Morphan, symbolizing the independent gunslinger of the romanticized Old West, lives in a demobilized '51 Chevrolet convertible. It sits without tires by the side of the highway surrounded by "garbage, tin cans, cardboard boxes, Coca-Cola bottles and other junk." In *Cowboy Mouth* (1971), the entire set serves as a metaphor for this disappointment and loss. A small room filled with images of the past — pictures of old-time cowboys, letters, and stuffed dolls — are mingled with images of a lost mobility or means of escape — travel posters, old tires, and license plates from Southern states.

In his essay "Explore," Shepard notes, "All the land has been discovered. . . . Now the move is inner space." The exploration of this new frontier in his plays, of the "inner space" of his characters, especially with regard to the male, consistently involves the dangerous confrontation with the demons of the self. This inner exploration, as his primary characters attempt to define the private self, the individuals they are, versus the public self, that identity inherited from family and community, and their ultimate and even inevitable failure to do so becomes a thematic through-line in Shepard's plays.

KEY INFLUENCES AND STYLE

The Rhythms of Language and Image

Shepard was an actor and a musician before becoming a playwright and director. His writing is heavily influenced by the rhythm of jazz, having listened, from early boyhood, to his father's jazz records. In addition, his father, a drummer, taught Shepard how to play drums. At the Village Gate where Shepard worked in the 1960s, he was exposed to legendary jazz artists, which further influenced his own playing. Later musical influences included rock, country, and bluegrass. Throughout his playwriting career, Shepard has remained involved in music — playing and recording with the Holy Modal Rounders and others and touring with Bob Dylan's Rolling Thunder Revue. He currently plays gigs with his son, Walker.

Unique, too, is Shepard's being a "primitive" early on: He was never schooled in traditional dramatic theory and structure. This naïveté led Shepard, especially in his early plays, to integrate the aforementioned elements of pop mythology into his dramatic writing. Shepard's early influences were heavily visual as well, which led him to create plays in which the meaning of image is equal to the meaning conveyed by dialogue. His primitivism and the influences of music and film resulted in Shepard's unique theatrical style, a synthesis of the rhythms of language and image, which was different both from Realism and from the nonrealistic styles of other theatrical artists of the 1960s. As Ellen Oumano states in her biography, his plays communicate "not through the intellect but through the ear, like music, through the eye, like visual art, and through the heart," like myth.

Father and Son, Male and Female

On a biographical level, perhaps the most powerful influence on Shepard's writing was his problematic relationship with his father, a distant man, ultimately an alcoholic recluse. Over and over again in his plays, Shepard explores the conflicted relationship between father and son, which erupts, finally, in a battle for supremacy and definition within the dysfunctional family unit. As if there were not enough room within that unit for both, one must destroy the other or be absorbed by him. Again and again, the father is depicted in his plays as distant, drinking, and periodically abandoning the family. In the later plays, the inability of the son, despite repeated efforts, to reconcile with the father is pronounced.

Shepard's perception of the female and the relationship between male and female is also a powerful influence on his writing. The sexes are depicted as irreparably polarized, drawn to each other but ultimately so diametrically distinct in emotion and psychology that only a temporary union is possible. The playwright once described this relationship as "terrible and impossible."

AMERICAN ROMANTIC

Shepard's view of American society is based on an awareness of the massive social, political, and psychological changes that have happened in the United States since the American Civil War. Before that conflict, Shepard — indeed the Romantic Movement in general — imagined America to be a land of "rugged individualism," which included the exploration and settlement of the western frontier. Before the Civil War, the United States, though grounded in unified communities and families, still saw the value of and need for the solitary, individual hero.

In this view, Shepard demonstrates that he is undoubtedly an American Romantic in both style and theme. What he and other Romantics share is an emphasis on the individual's connection to the land and nature and the strong feeling that if this connection is lost, humankind will suffer until it is somehow regained. They stress the value of the individual and especially the hero and the actions of the hero versus a corrupt or restrictive society.

Shepard, like the Romantics, uses folk heroes as symbols. As in the Romantic tradition, Shepard makes great use of myth in the structure and images of his plays. He shares their emphasis on the theme of freedom versus conformity or societal restriction and their belief in the inherent superiority of intuition over reason and of subjective over objective reality. In his later plays, he furthermore expresses the belief in the spiritual superiority of the female.

But Shepard is a qualified or disappointed Romantic. The hero is seen as the potential savior of a weak society, but like the later Romantics of the nineteenth century, Shepard is painfully aware of how even a weak society is important to the individual, and conflict in his plays often devolves upon the attempts of the hero/individual to integrate with society. Thematic resolution is absent in his plays because, to the playwright, the human personality is inevitably dualistic, even schizophrenic. Integration or synthesis is impossible or ultimately destructive, and the quest for Romantic "wholeness" or unity is doomed to failure from the beginning. The myth is proven to be defunct, the hero ultimately unheroic; the female survives without the male.

In Shepard's one-act play *Action*, written in 1975, the year the United States ended two decades of military involvement in the Vietnam War, a character named Jeep recounts a meeting between Walt Whitman, the great American poet, and Abraham Lincoln at the start of the Civil War. In Jeep's recounting, the poet is a witness to lost expectations; the beginning of the war signals the loss of American innocence. The other characters in the play do not know who Walt Whitman was, and the play implies that Whitman, indeed modern America, was disappointed in its own Romantic expectations. Shepard is the inheritor of both a frontier Romanticism and of a post–world war cynicism and hopelessness. His themes reflect as well the post-1950s disappointment in a mechanized, consumer culture with its resultant cultural and individual alienation from self and other. His dramaturgy reveals the influence of Romanticism with its goal of intuitive and emotional impact, but this is blended with the use of the techniques of Expressionism, Absurdism, and Existentialism — artistic movements that were generated by the horrors witnessed during World Wars I and II.

THE EARLY AND LATER PLAYS

Critics divide Shepard's canon into two periods: the early plays and the later or family plays. *Curse of the Starving Class* (1978) is cited as marking the transition from early to later.

However, Shepard's themes and his experimentation with stylistic combinations are consistent from the early *Cowboys* to the present. The later plays show a more sophisticated combination of Realism and surrealism and a stronger development of character, but it is in the early plays that he established a "vocabulary" of images and themes and a dramatic technique that became a kind of code to his work.

No Escape

As previously stated, the difficulty of defining the self is a central, recurring theme in Shepard's dramas. His characters in their efforts to become unique, independent individuals repeatedly come in conflict with society. Each character attempts to define his or her self as a unique, private "me" and then futilely tries to synthesize this newly defined self with the public self. The public self is a collective identity, defined but also limited by both the culture or society and the family through psychological and biological inherited traits. Shepard's plays dramatize how it is impossible to reconcile the past (inheritance) with the present — the freedom to act and create or preserve the self.

Indeed, the "presentness of the past" is menacing in Shepard's plays. The individual personality is in constant danger of being absorbed by the past even as the individual searches for his or her own identity, for a wholeness through integrating the self with his or her inheritance. In the early plays, the self is defined only through rebellion against repressive influences, not through the community or family. The individual, often symbolized as an artist, attempts to establish a separate identity or self by separating and escaping from the family and community, but he or she is invariably unsuccessful. Separation cannot be successful in Shepard's world, where a ruthless and vicious social and biological Darwinism prevails. To survive, society, often symbolized by the family, needs the individual to be the inheritor and carrier of history and culture and so must kill the individual's unique self. As Shepard notes in his prose work, *Motel Chronicles*, there is no escape from family and society. He reverses the traditional function of society and family as a support system; instead, it is dangerous and destructive.

Integration or Absorption

Shepard's plays evolved from the individual attempting total separation from the family and society (early plays) to attempted social synthesis (later plays). First is the need to escape then the realization that escape is impossible leading to the attempt to integrate and become a whole personality. His plays dramatize the impossibility both of total self-creation and of synthesis or wholeness. Integration in the family or society, which also signifies the past or inheritance, is possible only through one family member displacing another, such as the son replacing the father. But in this process, the son becomes completely absorbed into the family and culture, losing his original unique identity. Individual characteristics are lost in this terrible "metamorphosis," a transformation in which the self is lost, absorbed by the past and by the psychological and biological influences it sought first to escape and later to integrate.

In the early plays, Shepard began examining the Oedipal complex, the archetypal conflict between father and son, which continues through the later or family plays. In the early plays, this conflict symbolizes the larger and more abstract conflict between self (the son) and society (the father). The dramas depict the son's search for the father, his attempt at reconciliation with the patriarch, and his realization that father and son cannot exist simultaneously. Only one can survive, not both. In an act of self-preservation, the son attempts to destroy the father but ultimately becomes him as those characteristics acquired during the period of self-creation are annihilated, and the son surrenders completely to the fatalism of his heredity.

THE ROCK GARDEN

The Rock Garden (1964) is a striking summary of the themes, images, and style in Shepard's early period that continued and evolved in the later plays. According to Oumano, Shepard stated that *The Rock Garden* "is about leaving my mom and dad," but the play reveals a far greater subtext. The distant father and rivalry between father and son as well as the dysfunctional bond between mother and son are present. Also depicted is the simultaneous affection and hostility between the frequently absent husband and dissatisfied wife, and the son's instinct to emulate the father while protecting the mother.

Stylistically minimal, *The Rock Garden* is predominantly nonrealistic. The characters are depersonalized, labeled Woman, Boy, Girl, and Man, which suggests a universal dysfunctional family. Time is ambiguous; the scenes depict a progressive deterioration of familial relationships, but how much time elapses between each scene is not indicated. The play's three scenes develop from three separate images, each carefully dictated by Shepard in staging, lighting, and sound directions, that express the triangular conflict between father, mother, and son.

Scene One establishes the theme of familial isolation. A generic dinner table is set center on an otherwise empty stage. The Man sits at its head, reading a magazine, and his two teenage children sit on either side. There is no dialogue — in the play silence is often juxtaposed with dialogue/monologue — and no action distracts from the thematic focus. Shepard presents the American family as an image without substance, a concept of contemporary vacuousness he depicts in visual metaphor frequently. The mother is missing; interaction is nonexistent. The father seems oblivious to the children, and they seem to want, but fear, attention. The Girl spills her milk, and lights black out.

Scene Two, set in a bedroom, reveals the developing estrangement between mother and son. The son is focused on his mother, referred to as "the Woman" from his depersonalized perspective, and the mother's subtle but continuous emasculation of the son reveals her displaced hostility toward him. The Woman lies in bed under several blankets, and the Boy sits in a rocking chair (another recurring image) dressed in underwear. The Boy's presence in his parents' bedroom dressed in underwear suggests his willingness to take the father's place — especially since the father takes the same chair dressed the same way at the scene's end. The Woman compares the Boy to her father, identifying similar unattractive physical features, and suggests that her son also inherited unattractive qualities from his father. When she asks him to get her water and, later, blankets, the Boy quietly complies but returns wearing pants. The Woman notes that his toes, like her father's, are odd; the Boy leaves to get her another blanket and returns wearing shoes. This action is repeated until the Boy has finally retreated under an overcoat. The father passes the window dressed in a hat and overcoat, which associates him with the son, now similarly dressed. The Boy runs offstage, and the Man enters dressed in underwear and sits in the chair, rocking; he attempts conversation, but the Woman responds in monosyllables. There is a long silence as the Man rocks, and the lights dim slowly.

Scene Three depicts the son's growing hostility to and challenge of the father's superiority. Lights come up on a bare stage with a couch downstage left and a chair upstage right. The Boy sits on the chair facing upstage so that his back is to the Man on the couch, which visually communicates the emotional distance between them. Both are dressed in underwear. The father attempts to involve the son in the repair of the house and garden, offering the possibility of mutual respect, but the son rejects the offer in favor of a relationship in which he is dominant. Shepard specifies the "Boy never turns to address the man but delivers all his lines into the air." Three times in the scene as the father talks "the Boy nods out from boredom and falls off his chair," and "the Man goes on oblivious." The father describes the activities they can share, especially the construction of the rock garden, and the son states that "when I come it's like a river." He describes the volume of his ejaculations, the more satisfying sexual positions, and the most desirable physical characteristics of women. The Man falls from the couch, and the play ends.

THE HOLY GHOSTLY

Shepard's work portrays contemporary life in dualistic terms: self versus other; male versus female; art versus commercialism; instinct versus intellect; West versus East; the private versus the collective; the past versus the present and future. He uses Native American culture, frequently Hopi culture, as an example of cultural wholeness and functional synthesis of past and present. Old West and Native American imagery are notable in *The Holy Ghostly* (1970), another seminal play in Shepard's canon and a clear illustration of the focus in the early plays.

The Holy Ghostly, slightly over twice the length of *The Rock Garden*, dramatically extends the exploration of the father/son conflict. The title refers to the mystic triangle of Father, Son, and Holy Ghost. The father is Stanley (Pop); the son is Ice who has changed his name from Stanley Hewitt Moss VII; the Holy Ghost is the Chindi who tracks down and carries off those who are dead but unaware of it. The play is set in the desert in the Badlands at night. A large campfire is center stage: Fire becomes the symbol of the father, used for a final image of his resurrection through destruction.

The play opens with Ice toasting marshmallows for the old man, much like the son in *The Rock Garden* providing the mother with water and blankets. But though Ice tries, like *The Rock Garden* son, to appease his hostile parent by submissively providing for him, his name connotes a coldness toward his father, and ice is developed as the symbol in opposition to fire. Pop wakes and points his gun at Ice, a strong visual expression of the escalating hostility between them. Pop treats Ice like a child and responds to respect with contempt, deriding his son's musical success; his envy of and refusal to acknowledge Ice's accomplishments are the initial source of conflict.

To escape the father's influence, Ice left for New York and changed his name. Pop sees this as a betrayal and insists on calling Ice "Stanley." He asked his son to return to the Badlands to help fight the Chindi but treats the event as the son's "rite of passage." To prove his maturity, Ice suggests an immediate confrontation with the ghost; he draws his gun and runs into the darkness.

The Chindi enters, and Pop recognizes it as Ice. When he attempts to kill the Chindi, it disappears, and Pop shouts after it, first offering reconciliation then a warning: "If that's the way you want it that's the way you'll get it." He later assembles and loads a bazooka. Drum beats begin, identified with the Native American–influenced characterization of the Chindi, as Pop describes the hardships he has endured and the joy he felt returning from war and learning his first son had been born.

Ice enters with the drum and war paint on his face, saying, "I saw the Chindi, Pop . . . He told me that you were dead and you don't even know it." He threatens to kill Pop if he continues to call him Stanley, insisting that his father acknowledge his self-creation. Ice has become a man, but to complete the rite of passage, he must destroy the genetic and cultural bond or be destroyed.

However, Shepard indicates the son usurping the father's role is simply role reversal. The Witch, the Chindi's "old lady," enters carrying a corpse that looks exactly like the father and tells Pop that when the body has completely stiffened he will know he is dead. Through the Witch, Shepard expresses a recurring concern: the psychological, emotional, and spiritual fragmentation of the American individual and the vital need for synthesis. But father and son reject synthesis; they reverse roles several times until Pop becomes like a little boy, and Ice becomes like his father. The old man cuddles in his son's lap, and Ice tells a story that underscores the unresolvable conflict of dualism and the fatalistic nature of biological and cultural inheritance.

In the story, the world is created through the collision between a "super sun" and a "giant ice planet." The ice planet was buried within the sun where it incubated and ultimately exploded. A fragment became the earth, and "[e]ver since then the earth has been carrying on a constant struggle between fire and ice." Pop refuses to accept the story and reverts to the dominant role. Like the father in *The Rock Garden*, Pop tries to reconcile with Ice, but only to effect his own rebirth, a form of immortality Ice will not allow. Pop reminds him that "[t]here must have been some time once when you needed me and I helped you out . . . Well, now you can pay me back." Silently, Ice draws his gun, shoots Pop, and walks into the darkness.

However, the inheritance will haunt the son despite all attempts to destroy or escape it. Pop acknowledges that he is dead then realizes he is not bleeding and can walk into the fire without injury. The play ends with Pop dancing through the fire, his element. He is reborn through the son. Shepard presents the inescapable union of Father, Son, and Holy Ghost — the patriarch, the child, and the bond of genetics and culture.

Shepard wrote the play for staging in the round, reinforcing the inevitably circular and doomed struggle for definition, and he emphasizes the initial visual by dictating a slow fade up of light. The dream desert environment is created only through language and action. Dialogue underscores the nonrealistic handling of time and space, and stage properties are oversized, appearing from nowhere when a character needs them. The final visual and aural image reinforces the negative resolution. The Chindi's bells, "a live sound," and drum resonate as Pop dances in the fire, and finally "the whole theater is consumed in flames."

CURSE OF THE STARVING CLASS

With *Curse of the Starving Class* in 1978, Shepard begins to use the "domestic drama formula" as a frame of reference for the audience. In what becomes a consistent technique, Shepard first presents normalcy (Realism), which then goes wrong (the absurd). The initial image of normalcy, of a domestic drama, which is then deliberately destroyed, devolving into surreal, violent images, becomes all the more disturbing. As will recur in *True West* (1980), the kitchen, the archetypal American family room, is transformed through destruction into the surreal. However in *Curse of the Starving Class*, unlike *True West* and other later works such as *Buried Child* (1978) and *Fool for Love* (1983), the absurd dominates the blend of realistic and nonrealistic elements. Before the play starts, the father has kicked in the kitchen door and the floor is littered with its fragments. Later, the floor will be littered with food and finally with the carcass of a slaughtered lamb.

Curse of the Starving Class extends the exploration of dysfunctional individuals and families to implicate a class and ultimately a nation. The title refers to a social group, or society as a whole, starving for a viable identity in an increasingly empty culture. The family's empty refrigerator is a central image, and the reference is reinforced when the father prepares the traditional American breakfast as if it will bring salvation. The "curse" or "family poison" is genetic inheritance. To the mother and later to Wesley, her son, it is the fatalism of biology and karma: "Something in the blood. Hereditary. Highly explosive."

During the play, the parents make individual attempts to sell their property and escape, the mother to Europe, and the father, Weston, who already disappears periodically, to Mexico. Emma, the daughter, like her father, hopes for escape to and anonymity in Mexico; she does not understand the nature of the "family poison" but realizes she cannot escape it and decides to exploit the curse in a life of crime. Wesley is the focal character who fantasizes about escaping to Alaska but recognizes the value in the family and their land. The play depicts Wesley's struggle against the disintegration of his family and loss of his home and his final resignation to accept the curse as inevitable.

Empty Refrigerator, Futile Lives

Shepard describes the set as a typical family kitchen but lacking details and logic. A table with four mismatched chairs sits upstage center; "suspended in midair" stage left and right are red-checked curtains. There is a refrigerator and stove, and the remains of the door the father has destroyed are placed down right. Act One presents the central images, conflicts, and themes that will be developed in the following two acts.

Wesley tries to clean up the mess his drunken, absent father made the night before and to defend his father's actions. Each character repeatedly opens the refrigerator door, stares into it, and finds it empty. The mother, Ella, and daughter, Emma, argue over whether they "belong to the Starving Class," with Ella taking the position that "[w]e're hungry, and that's starving enough for me." Ella tells her children that she's working with a lawyer to sell the family property, an avocado ranch, to wealthy developers, offering them a chance to escape with her to Europe. Wesley argues that the property is valuable to the family and can be saved; he leaves. Emma tells her mother that she is escaping to Mexico instead.

Wesley returns with a live lamb suffering from maggots and sets it up in a pen center stage. Taylor, the lawyer, enters, and when Wesley tells him that his father will never sell the property, Taylor reveals that the father will have to sell because he is in terrible debt. Ella and Taylor leave just before the father, Weston, enters with what appears to be a bag of groceries. But the bag is actually full of artichokes, which the father purchased "for half-price" in the desert. The act ends with Weston telling his son that, without his wife's knowledge, he went into debt purchasing a piece of land in the desert, which turned out to be worthless. He tells Wesley that he's thinking of selling their ranch to purchase property in Mexico, then exits. The act ends with Wesley alone, staring at the lamb.

Cursed by a Poisonous Heritage

In Act Two, Shepard unites the metaphor of the "family poison" or curse, the fatalistically recurring biological and spiritual inheritance, with the visual image of the maggot-ridden lamb. Like the individual, family, and society, the lamb is rotting from the inside out. Weston says his outlook is "full of poison" and infected, and he tells his son that he recognized the poison in his own father: "I saw myself infected with it . . . His poison in my body . . . I didn't ask for it, but I got it." The tragedy of the play is that individuals, family, and culture could be saved but are lost; the property, though it needs repair, is clearly valuable — two outside characters vie to acquire it for commercial exploitation. Dispossession does not result from victimization but from passivity, a self-destructive quality the parents pass down to the children.

The Impossibility of Rebirth

Act Three opens with Weston apparently reborn. He has awakened sober, ready to forget the past. He has cleaned the kitchen, done the laundry, bathed, and changed his clothes. A fresh pot of coffee is brewing on the stove. Weston tells his son that he suddenly realizes what it means to have roots, own property, and be the head of a family. He has thrown away his old, soiled clothes (and with them he thinks his old life and its consequences), taken a hot then a cold bath, shaved, and put on clean clothes. Weston does not understand that the property is no longer his. His debts are still outstanding, and he cannot be reborn after a baptism in his own dirty bath water. Rebirth is, in Shepard's universe, impossible.

Tragically, the father realizes too late that there are positive aspects to property ownership and family — aspects that have been clear to the son all along. Weston relates to his son how he made his new discovery: "I felt like I knew you through the flesh and blood. Like our bodies were connected and we could never escape that. But I didn't feel like escaping. I felt like it was a good thing . . . That a family wasn't just a social thing . . . It was a reason of nature that we were all together under the same roof. Not that we had to be but that we were supposed to be . . . I started feeling full of hope." Wesley responds, "I'm starving."

Later in the act, Emma returns to find Wesley in his father's dirty, discarded clothes, eating ravenously from the refrigerator and from scraps on the floor. She tells him he will end up just like his father, "diseased." Wesley has butchered and eaten the lamb. The slaughtered lamb symbolizes the sacrifice of the son: his loss of innocence and the father's rebirth through the son (as in the metaphoric rebirth of the father in *The Holy Ghostly*). There is subsequently no place for Weston in the family. Wesley coldly tells him that he is in danger due to his unpaid debts and firmly tells him to leave for Mexico, which the displaced father does.

Upon seeing Wesley in his father's clothes, Ella refers to him as Weston and to Emma as his daughter. Wesley has been absorbed, gone backward, but unlike his sister, who is killed in her attempt to escape the family, he has survived. The play implies that backward is the only path open to this dysfunctional family.

BURIED CHILD

Buried Child revisits the sins-of-the-father theme. In this play, Shepard uses psychological dissociation as a dramatic device to drive the action and combines the formulas of the prodigal son and a murder mystery to create a metarealistic style that almost seamlessly melds the surreal and real. In *Buried Child*, the need to synthesize past and present is fully developed. But the child referred to in the title, a murdered and buried baby, represents a dysfunctional synthesis. The baby was conceived incestuously (incestuous love appears again in *Fool for Love*). Its conception initiated the family's destruction in the play's prehistory, and its reappearance completes that destruction. Nature, an amoral force appearing as vegetation, becomes unavoidable karma: A lush growth of corn miraculously appears in the backyard, though the family did not plant it, and its eruption from the ground drives the hidden corpse of the child to the surface.

Shepard sets the play in Illinois, the state of his birth. By locating the play in the Midwestern corn belt, he identifies the dramatic action with America's "heartland." Corn functions as a major symbol: Native American and Aztec myth frequently associate corn with primal generative power and renewal and rebirth. The setting is a farm, once prosperous but now dilapidated (the condition of the family and nation); nothing has been planted "since about nineteen thirty-five." The characters are Dodge, the patriarch of the family who was once a successful farmer but is now an alcoholic, slovenly old man; his wife, Halie; and their sons Tilden, the oldest, and Bradley (a third son, Ansel, is spoken of but never appears). Appearing in Act Two are Vince, Tilden's son, and his girlfriend Shelly.

Religion, and its inability to provide aid for the family, is represented by Father Dewis, a man of the cloth in costume only, who appears for the first time in Act Three. Father Dewis shows a total lack of morality and gives poor guidance because it is easier. He and Halie arrive "slightly drunk," and he drinks during the ensuing action from a hip flask he shares with Halie. The two are having an affair and apparently spent the night together. Halie had left the house for her luncheon with Dewis in a black dress and hat, including veil, but returns the next day in a bright yellow dress and white gloves with her arms full of yellow roses.

Dodge, Halie, and the two sons are crippled by a mysterious past event. Bradley cut his leg off in a chainsaw accident and wears a wooden leg, the physical loss serving as a visual metaphor for his psychological state. Tilden is "profoundly burned out and displaced" and is treated like a gentle but overgrown child. He remembers fragments of the past only when his memory is triggered by outside stimulation. Dodge is nearly a complete invalid vulnerable to constant victimization by his sons. Dodge acknowledges the past only when it suits him, but his deliberate identification only with the present leaves him increasingly paralyzed. When he is finally cornered and confronted with the past in Act Three, Dodge reveals a detailed memory of the family history that gives him momentary power as he uses confession like a weapon against his wife and sons.

The increasing immobility and vulnerability of the male in general and the father in particular recurs frequently in Shepard's plays. When Dodge moves from the couch, he falls to the floor and is propped against the television. In *A Lie of the Mind* (1985), a father with bad feet, trapped in his armchair, needs his wife to put on his socks. In *Fool for Love*, the father is a ghost restricted to a rocking chair on a platform forward of the proscenium.

Living with but estranged from Dodge, Halie has placed her expectations on her sons. When they disappointed her (to some extent all pseudo-husbands will) and the baby was murdered, Halie constructed an idealized history that made the present livable. Ansel, the mystery son, may be Halie's idealized fiction based on the murdered baby. As all American sons should be, he was a war hero and basketball star, and Halie remembers that when Ansel died, she and Dodge were left alone: "Same as if they'd all died." She uses Ansel as a weapon to perpetuate her other sons' Oedipal attachment. Tilden's incestuous relationship to his mother gradually becomes clear; at the end, he carries the child's corpse to her room, the only character to visit her there other than Dewis. As for Bradley, Halie viciously exploits his fear of and devotion to her. Even her fantasy relationship with Ansel seems dysfunctional. He died, according to Halie, after marrying a woman of whom she disapproved, and Halie describes the unmaternal kiss she gave her son at his wedding.

Bradley is simultaneously the most unsympathetic and pathetic character in *Buried Child*. He regularly victimizes his father both to usurp his role and exact vengeance against him as a child murderer. In Act One, Dodge forbids Bradley's entrance to the house, refusing to acknowledge Bradley as his son; Bradley enters when his father is asleep and shaves Dodge's head until the scalp bleeds, symbolically castrating him. Bradley returns in Act Two and assaults each character present. Bradley drives Tilden out into the rainy night and symbolically rapes Shelly by forcing his fingers into her mouth, suggesting the extent of his neurosis in relation to women. In the final image of Act Two, he stands over his father and covers his head with Shelly's rabbit fur coat — in effect, "burying" him. When Act Three opens, Bradley has usurped his father's couch and blanket, but upon his mother's return becomes a whimpering baby, helpless without the wooden leg Shelly holds hostage as barter for the family history.

The entrance of Dodge's grandson, Vince, in Act Two, the "prodigal son" returning to rediscover his roots, is anticipated by Tilden's entrance in Act One, "his arms loaded with fresh ears of corn." He claims the backyard is full of corn, but Dodge and Halie refuse to believe it. Dodge orders him to put the corn back where it came from, and Tilden "dumps all the corn on Dodge's lap," indicating karmic nature's inescapable reaction to his crime. The family's refusal to acknowledge the growing vegetation is paralleled by their subsequent denial of any relationship to Vince, a denial that comes full circle in Vince's later assumption of Dodge's identity and denial of them. The first of three symbolic burials (two failed and one successful displacement) of Dodge closes Act One as Tilden gently buries his father in corn husks, spreading them "over the whole length of Dodge's body." This vegetative burial foreshadows nature's unearthing of the past and Dodge's death and resurrection through Vince.

One of Shepard's cowboy/artist characters, Vince wears cowboy boots (roots in American myth) and carries a saxophone (individual expression through art). Shelly is the outsider (Shepard's first use of the "witness" character), the catalyst to confession. Vince clearly anticipated the archetypal homecoming and is horrified when his family fails to recognize him. Dodge refuses to acknowledge he is anyone's grandfather, and Tilden tells Shelly, "I had a son once but we buried him." Vince leaves, ostensibly, to "put this all together" but, as is later revealed, planning to escape for good. Tilden tells Shelly he thought he "saw a face inside his face," referring, as Vince will in Act Three, to Vince's bone structure, which goes back indeterminate generations, a physical resemblance paralleling the reference to the genes and inheritance in *Curse*. Prompted by Shelly, Tilden reveals that Dodge drowned and buried the child, and this confrontation with the past cripples Dodge who lies helpless as Bradley arrives and assumes control. The act ends with the second burial of Dodge by Bradley, an "animal" burial that suggests no resurrection.

Act Three opens ironically with sunshine and singing birds as Dodge tells Shelly he in fact recognized Vince, but his grandson was of no consequence to him. The family gathers, and Shelly demands an explanation for their actions and the baby's murder. Dodge reveals that he remembers everything: Halie's child could not be his as he and Halie hadn't slept together for years; Tilden knew the identity of the father and had a close relationship with the baby. Dodge says, "We couldn't allow that to grow up right in the middle of our lives. It made everything we'd accomplished look like it was nothin'. . . I drowned it." He implies that Tilden and Halie had an incestuous relationship. The child was an unnatural union of past and present, of mother and son, which Dodge destroyed because it suggested his eldest son's almost successful displacement of him. His vengeance left Tilden "profoundly burned out and displaced." The patriarchal position will not pass to him or the crippled Bradley but to Vince. But it's a change only in "the age separatin' 'em," as Ice says, or only a "change of the guards," as Wesley puts it.

Vince returns violently, cutting his way through the porch screen to enter, "a murderer . . . who can devour whole families in a single gulp." He discovered, as he attempted to run, that he is inescapably defined by his roots, and he vows to pick up where his grandfather left off with the past as a blank slate. Only the strongest can survive, and the one who most resembles Dodge in his ruthlessness is Vince. As Dodge delivers a lyrical Last Will and Testament (resembling Pop's speech in *Ghostly*), leaving the house and all "paraphernalia therein" to his grandson, Vince ousts his uncle, throwing Bradley's wooden leg out the door as he crawls after it. Dodge dies, and Vince buries him for a final time with his blanket, placing Halie's roses on his chest.

Just as Wesley returns from his mysterious rite of passage in *Curse of the Starving Class* with a terrible resignation to his fate, Vince describes his transformation into the owner of the face Tilden saw inside his face, his absorption into the past generations of the family. He tells Dewis his plans to renovate the farm: "Start off on the ground floor." But Vince has also inherited the "paraphernalia therein," and when Dewis suggests that Vince look after his grandmother, Vince responds, "My grandmother? There's nobody else in this house." He reclines on the couch, his body assuming "the same relationship to Dodge," and Halie speaks from offstage, as she did at the opening, addressing Vince as her husband. In a speech ironically filled with images of fertility, she notes that the back lot is full of vegetables, as Tilden, holding the corpse of the child, "slowly makes his way up the stairs." The "return journey" metaphor is inverted, suggesting that negative growth is the only option. In final lines clearly evocative of Ibsen's *Ghosts* (another drama examining the inevitable return of the sins of the father), Halie remarks, "Maybe it's the sun. Maybe that's it. Maybe it's the sun."

EXPLORING THE ULTIMATE DUALITY

In Shepard's later work, the role of the female character assumes increased importance. From examining the individual within the context of family and society, his work progresses now to exploring the relationship between man and the woman — the ultimate duality. Shepard examines how the archetypal nature of the female possesses the potential both to oppose and balance the male. In this view, duality is both inevitable and potentially destructive.

About writing *Fool for Love* Shepard stated to Don Shewey, "I wanted to try to take this leap into a female character . . . it's hard for a man to say he can speak from the point of view of a woman." The following year he wrote the screenplay for *Paris, Texas*, a film that continues to examine the mysterious territory between male and female, and the year after that came *A Lie of the Mind*. In that play, Shepard indicates that the female may be capable of building a future; the male, whose undirected forces within himself turn destructive and cripple him, may not survive. According to Sessums, Shepard noted, "There's a sense that men have lost their place . . . And women seem very strong . . . they will continue to exist whether men are there or not . . . the female side . . . It's much more courageous than the male side." In 1988, Shepard wrote the screenplay for *Far North* about which he stated, "I'm absolutely fascinated by this female stuff right now, 'cause I'm beginning to realize that the female side knows so much more than the male side."

FOOL FOR LOVE

Fool for Love opens with Eddie and May in a cheap motel room on the outskirts of the Mojave Desert, where May lives. Eddie is trying to reconcile with May, his former lover, telling her he will never leave her again. May accuses him of having an affair with a rich woman and is conflicted about her feelings for Eddie. An Old Man in a rocking chair, who later turns out to be the father of both Eddie and May, is at first a silent witness to their conversation then later talks to both Eddie and May. He exists only in the minds of Eddie and May. Through the course of the play, the truth is gradually revealed that the Old Man (who is another distant, alcoholic father) had had an affair with May's mother, and that Eddie's mother committed suicide with the Old Man's shotgun when she discovered the adultery.

With May, Shepard begins a deeper examination of the female in relation to the male, which anticipates both Beth in *A Lie of the Mind* and Kate in *Far North*. May proves to be stronger in spirit than either her lover/half-brother Eddie or her father because she can, as can Beth and Kate, face the truth, live with it, and go on. At the end of the play, after listening to Eddie's and the Old Man's lyrical, romanticized fictional view of the past, May tells the stark, objective, and very ugly truth. Eddie is forced to admit that the father's actions in the past caused the suicide of his mother.

But the men can only briefly face the unglamorized truth. Eddie is doomed to repeat what his father did — drinking heavily and having relationships with two women. Shepard depicts their refusal to face the truth as weakness, grounded in their inability to connect with themselves, the world around them, or the other, the female. May can face the truth and reach out in empathy to the world or specifically to Eddie, but the gesture is futile. The men simply dissociate in avoidance and escape to their relative fictions. Eddie leaves May again to return to Hollywood and his rich mistress, and the Old Man returns to the "truth" of his marriage to Barbara Mandrell: "That's realism. I am actually married to Barbara Mandrell in my mind."

A LIE OF THE MIND

A Lie of the Mind balances the male and female roles in a manner unprecedented among Shepard's plays: There are four women to four men. Two of the women, Lorraine and Meg, are mother figures whose qualities have been seen in former plays (possessive and destructive, or a disoriented woman ineffective in defending her children against the father and the assaults of society and nature). One, Sally, is a sister figure, anticipated by Emma in *Curse of the Starving Class*. The major figure, and ultimately the protagonist of the play, is Beth, who has been brutally beaten and brain damaged by her husband, Jake, the son of Lorraine.

Jake's mother is a combination of Halie in *Buried Child* and Ella in *Curse of the Starving Class*. She was apparently unhappy with but inevitably attracted to her husband (an alcoholic who abandoned the family and was killed by a truck on a highway) and, like those two former characters, has shifted her expectations and affections to her son, Jake, even to excluding her other son and daughter, Frankie and Sally. Like Ella, Lorraine believes that the solution to her and the family's problems is escape, this time to Ireland in search of the roots that will bring identity. Similar to Halie, there is something unwholesome about her feelings toward Jake. She represents the terrible and destructive aspect of the feminine, especially the mother.

Meg, who is Beth and Mike's mother, still lives with her husband, Baylor. Although her unhappiness with her marriage has caused her to dissociate and to appear simple and weak, she is strong in her resolve to remain with her family and try to make it work. Baylor is gradually losing his mobility. He spends more and more time in his armchair and depends increasingly on Meg, whom he criticizes constantly. His wife must massage his weakening feet and help him take off his boots and put on his socks. In one episode during which Meg tends to her husband while he impatiently reviles her, Meg reveals the female's ability to see beneath the surface, to understand both the male and female issues. In this exchange, Shepard painfully exposes the obtuseness and disconnected weakness of the modern male:

> MEG: The female — the female one needs — the other.
> BAYLOR: What other?

MEG: The male. The male one.

BAYLOR: Oh.

MEG: But the male one — doesn't really need the other. Not the same way.

BAYLOR: I don't get ya.

MEG: The male one goes off by himself. Leaves. He needs something else. But he doesn't know what it is. He doesn't really know what he needs. So he ends up dead. By himself.

Sally, the sister, is a version of the modern, self-sufficient woman who possesses both strength and compassion, first seen in Shelly in *Curse of the Starving Class*. She is able to see the truth — in her relationships and in the consequences of actions — and to live with that truth. Sally is capable of living with and helping her mother to cope, despite her mother's antagonism to her daughter who she perceives as a rival female.

Beth is the lover and the seer who eventually leads Jake to a heightened if limited and temporary awareness of the nature of love and the relationship of male and female. Her beating by Jake, who is irrationally jealous, has enabled her to see clearly what went wrong between her and Jake and what needs to happen in a male-female relationship. Beth tells Jake's brother, Frankie:

> Look how big a man is. So big. He scares himself. His shirt scares him. He puts his scary shirt on so it won't scare himself. He can't see it when it's on him. Now he thinks it's him . . . Now, I'm like the man. *(Pumps her chest up, closes her fists, sticks her chin out and struts in the shirt.)* Just like the man. Shirt brings me a man. I am a shirt man. Can you see? Like father. You see me? Like brother . . . Between us we can make a life. You could be the woman. You be . . . Maybe you could be him. Pretend. Maybe. Just him. Just like him. But soft. With me. Gentle. Like a woman-man . . . You could be better. Better man. Maybe. Without hate. You could be my

sweet man. You could. Pretend to be. Try. My sweetest man . . . You could pretend so much that you start thinking this is me. You could really fall in love with me. How would that be. In a love we never knew.

In the play, the men are in rather serious trouble, with the exception of Frankie, the "witness" character who listens to the others' confessions. Baylor's increasing helplessness and resulting unpleasantness as well as his inability both to perceive and accept the truth anticipate the future for both Jake and Mike, who have already begun to exhibit the same symptoms. The women, on the other hand, progress. Beth has carried the compassionate vision of her mother further. Sally and Lorraine find that despite their past hostility, they can work together to build a future. The men do not progress in the play but decline: They cannot understand themselves, each other, or the world around them. The resulting fate of the male, the lonely death in the wilderness foreseen by Meg, is realized in Shepard's next play, *Far North.*

TRUE WEST

True West play displays many of the themes that run through Shepard's canon as well as some familiar characters: the alcoholic, absent, and indifferent father and the ineffective, somewhat vacuous mother. But in *True West,* the relationship between father and son is replaced by a battle between Lee and his younger brother Austin. This play also examines the reality versus the myth of the true West.

The contemporary West is embodied foremost by Austin, the civilized Hollywood screenwriter who is house-sitting for his mother while she is on vacation in Alaska. The mother's suburban home; the chirping crickets in the background, specified in the stage directions; Saul, the Hollywood producer; and the freeways and Safeways are all emblematic of this overcivilized, packaged West. This West is a mirage, an irrigated desert ready to return to arid wilderness if untended — as the mother's unwatered houseplants do and as Austin himself does, later in the play, when his veneer of control strips away to reveal a savage anger. It is as superficial as the movies Saul produces.

The romanticized West is represented by Lee's proposed screenplay, "a true to life western." The story interests Saul who sees the real West in it because it is, conversely, the West of cinematic myth. Austin is initially pleased that Saul wants to produce his brother's screenplay, until he discovers that Saul has dropped Austin's project in favor of Lee's. But he agrees to help write a treatment of Lee's screenplay if Lee will take him to the desert when they are done. He tells Lee he wants to learn the desert's secrets, saying, "There's nothin' real down here, Lee!" He yearns for the vital struggles Lee endures alone in the desert, seeing them as more "real" than his own in suburbia.

To Austin, Lee's screenplay is "a bullshit story," but Lee needs the myth because he struggles to survive on the real desert that bears no resemblance to Hollywood's West. Lee envies his brother, his identity and lifestyle as a Yale-educated writer with a home, wife, and children.

Lee represents the true West, which is neither romantic nor glamorous. Lee tries to destroy Austin's romantic delusion, telling his brother he is living out there because he can't make it in the civilized West. The true West is a barren desert identified with the howl of coyotes, which overwhelms the chirping crickets. In this environment, Lee must scrounge for survival, earning money by fighting his dog or thieving. The true West is most poignantly represented by the brothers' alcoholic, impoverished father.

True West also examines the theme of the artist versus the nonartist and the artist confronted by commercialism. Austin yearns for the physical life of Lee, and Lee for the creative life Austin's writing allows him. The action of the play proceeds from Lee's decision to take over Austin's identity by usurping his relationship with Saul, just as he initially usurps the territory of their mother's home.

The brothers are opposites, desperate to achieve completeness. But the impulse for synthesis is doomed to disappointment. The play ends with Lee and Austin engaged in a vicious fight as Lee tries to leave Austin behind, and Austin, emotionally stripped to his animal essence, tries to strangle Lee with a telephone cord. In a powerfully expressive final image, the brothers face off as a lone coyote howls in the distance. As lights "fade softly into moonlight, the figures of the brothers now appear to be caught in a vast desert-like landscape."

Mom, who enters near the end, is a fully dissociated "cartoon" stripped to essential qualities in contrast to the realistic handling of Austin and Lee. She returns disoriented by her journey into the "unknown" of Alaska and cannot make sense of the fight raging between her sons nor of the ruins of her kitchen. Mom believes Picasso is in town (the civilization she needs after confronting the wilderness), although Austin tries to explain that Picasso is dead. Unable to control her sons and unfamiliar with the environment they have created, she leaves for a hotel and the Picasso exhibit, saying, "I can't stay here. This is worse than being homeless."

AT PRESENT

After three decades of prolific writing and directing, Shepard concentrated on his film and television career for some years, garnering an Oscar nomination for his performance in *The Right Stuff.* The years 2005–09 have marked a return for Shepard to prose writing with *Great Dream of Heaven* (2002) and to his dramas with *The God of Hell* (2004), *Kicking a Dead Horse* (2007), and *Ages of the Moon* (2009).

DRAMATIC MOMENTS

from the Major Plays

These short excerpts are from the playwright's major plays. They give a taste of the work of the playwright. Each has a short introduction in brackets that helps the reader understand the context of the excerpt. The excerpts, which are in chronological order, illustrate the main themes mentioned in the In an Hour essay.

from COWBOY MOUTH (1971)

CHARACTERS

Slim
Cavale

[The one-act *Cowboy Mouth* contains numerous themes and techniques that are quintessentially Shepard. Two realistic characters with symbolic names, Slim (the cowboy, the seemingly independent self with strong roots in the past) and Cavale (from a French word that means "escape" or "on the run," a self-created identity) struggle to define themselves. A mythic figure, Lobster Man, appears as the "Rock and Roll Savior," apparently the ultimate self-creator. Surrealism, Absurdism, and Realism are blended in a nearly balanced synthesis; the first two-thirds of the play are largely realistic and the final third surrealistic, anticipating the structure of the later plays.

In this excerpt, Slim and Cavale reveal their willingness to remake reality and themselves to create a workable relationship and to find the happiness that alludes them. They discuss the nature of the rock-and-roll religion and its savior, and Slim reveals his inability to put his past behind him so that he can become that savior. The entire one-act takes place in the one-room apartment Slim and Cavale share.]

A fucked-up bed center stage. Raymond, a dead crow, on the floor. Scattered all around on the floor is miscellaneous debris: hubcaps, an old tire, raggedy costumes, a boxful of ribbons, lots of letters, a pink telephone, a bottle of Nescafé, a hot plate. Seedy wallpaper with pictures of cowboys peeling off the wall. Photographs of Hank Williams and Jimmie Rodgers, stuffed dolls, crucifixes. License plates from southern states nailed to the wall. Travel poster of Panama. A funky set of drums, to one side of the stage. An electric guitar and amplifier on the other side. Rum, beer, white lightning, Sears catalogue.

Cavale has kidnapped Slim off the streets with an old .45. She wants to make him into a rock-and-roll star, but they fall in love. We find them after one too many mornings. They're both mean as snakes. Slim is charging around screaming words; Cavale is rummaging through junk, yelling with a cracked throat. The lights come up on them in this state.

SLIM: Cavale?

CAVALE: Yeah?

SLIM: How come we're so unhappy?

CAVALE: Must be the time of year.

SLIM: Yeah. It's that time of year, all right. That must be it. Maybe we could change it.

CAVALE: What?

SLIM: The time of year. Let's change the time of year to Indian summer. That's my favorite time of year. What's your favorite time of year?

CAVALE: Fall.

SLIM: Okay, we'll change the time of year to fall. Okay?

CAVALE: Okay.

SLIM: Okay, now it's fall. Are you happy?

CAVALE: Yeah.

SLIM: Good. Now tell me a story.

CAVALE: Stop asking me that. I can't tell no stories unless I'm inspired. Who wants to listen to something uninspired?

SLIM: Okay, then tell me what it means to be a rock-and-roll star. Tell me that. I'm supposed to be a rock-and-roll star. You're going to make me into a rock-and-roll star, right?

CAVALE: Right.

SLIM: So tell me what it means, so I'll have something to go by.

CAVALE: Well, it's hard, Slim. I'll try to tell you but you gotta stay quiet. You gotta let me fish around for the right way to tell ya'. I always felt the rhythm of what it means but I never translated it to words. Here, hold Raymond. Come on. It's like, well, the highest form of anything is sainthood. A marvelous thief like Villon or Genet . . . they were saints 'cause they raised thievery to its highest state of grace. Ole George Carter, black and beat to shit on some dock singing "Rising River Blues" . . . he was one. He sang like an ole broke-down music box. Some say Jesse James was one . . . and me . . . I dream of being one. But I can't. I mean I can't be the saint people dream of now. People want a street angel. They want a saint but with a cowboy mouth. Somebody to get off on when they can't bet off on themselves. I think that's what Mick Jagger is trying to do . . . what Bob Dylan seemed to be for a while. A sort of god in our image . . . ya' know? Mick Jagger came close but he got too conscious. For a while he gave me hope . . . but he misses. He's not whole. Hey Slim . . . am I losing ya'? I mean, just tell me if I'm getting draggy. It's just hard and it's real important.

SLIM: No baby, it's beautiful.

CAVALE: Well, I want it to be perfect, 'cause it's the only religion I got. It's like . . . well, in the old days people had Jesus and those guys to embrace . . . they created a god with all their belief energies . . . and when they didn't dig themselves they could lose themselves in the Lord. But it's too hard now. We're earthy people, and the old saints just don't make it, and the old God is just too far away. He don't represent our pain no more. His words don't shake through us no more. Any great motherfucker rock-'n'-roll song can raise me higher than all of Revelations. We created rock-'n'-roll from our own image, it's our child . . . a child that's gotta burse in the mouth of a savior . . . Mick Jagger would love to be that savior but it ain't him. It's like . . . the savior . . . rocking to Bethlehem to be born. Ya' know what I mean, Slim?

SLIM: Well, fuck it, man, I ain't no savior.

CAVALE: But you've got it. You've got the magic. You could do it. You could be it.

SLIM: How?

CAVALE: You gotta collect it. You gotta reach out and grab all the little broken, busted-up pieces of people's frustration. That stuff in them that's lookin' for a way out or a way in. You know what I mean? The stuff in them that makes them wanna' see God's face. And then you gotta take all that into yourself and pour it back out. Give it back to them bigger than life. You gotta be unselfish, Slim. Like God was self-ish, He kept Himself hid. He wasn't a performer. You're a performer, man. You gotta be like a rock-and-roll Jesus with a cowboy mouth.

SLIM: You fucking cunt!

(He jumps up and starts tearing the place apart, throwing things against the walls and screaming his head off.)

SLIM: You stupid fucking cunt! Two years ago or one year ago! If it was then! If this was happening to me then, I could've done it! I could've done it! But not now! Not fucking now! I got another life! I can't do it now! It's too late! You can't bring somebody's dream up to the surface like that! It ain't fair! It ain't fucking fair! I know I could do it, but you're not supposed to tempt me! You're twisting me up! You're tearing me inside out! Get out of my house! Get the fuck out of my house!

CAVALE: This ain't your house. This is my house.

SLIM: It's nobody's house. Nobody's house.

(He collapses, exhausted from his violence. Cavale goes to him as if to soothe him, then realizes it's her dream being busted and not his. She starts yelling at him while he just lies there wiped out.)

CAVALE: You're fucking right — nobody's house. A little nobody with a big fucking dream. Her only dream. My only dream. I spread my dreams at your feet, everything I believe in, and you tread all over them with your simpy horseshit. Fuck you. Fuck you. Poor, poor baby. I take your world and shake it. Well, you took my fantasy and shit on it. I was doing the streets looking for a man with nothing so I could give him everything. Everything it takes to make the world reel like a drunkard. But you have less than nothing, baby, you have part of a thing. And it's settled. And if it's settled I can't do nothing to alter it. I can't do shit. I can't give you nothing. I can't. I can't. You won't let me.

****

from **CURSE OF THE STARVING CLASS** (1978)

from Act Three

CHARACTERS

Ella
Weston
Wesley

[This excerpt from Act Three, the final act, takes place in the kitchen, the sole set for the entire play. Both the mother, Ella, and the father, Weston, without the knowledge of the other, have attempted to sell the family's avocado ranch and house. Neither Weston nor Ella realize that Weston has already lost the property due to his rising and unpaid debts. Weston, like so many fathers depicted in Shepard's plays, returned to the family the night before, drunk, after a long absence. In the morning, Weston attempted to "resurrect" himself, taking a hot then cold bath, eating the all-American breakfast of bacon and eggs, and washing the family's laundry. Here, Ella has just returned from jail where she was visiting Emma, the daughter, who was arrested for shooting up the Alibi Club owned by Ellis. A sick lamb is in a pen center stage, put there originally by Wesley, who was nursing it, then returned by Weston, who is still trying to save the lamb.]

Ella enters from stage right. She looks haggard and tired. She stands there looking at Weston, who keeps cooking the eggs. Then she looks at the lamb. Weston knows she's there but doesn't look at her.

ELLA: *(After pause.)* What's that lamb doing back in here?

WESTON: I got him back on his feet. It was nip and tuck there for a while. Didn't think he's pull through. Maggots clear up into the small intestine.

ELLA: *(Crossing to table.)* Spare me the details.

(She pulls off her white gloves and sits exhausted into the chair at stage right. She looks at the piles of clean laundry.)

WESTON: *(Still cooking.)* Where you been anyway?

ELLA: Jail.

WESTON: Oh, they finally caught ya', huh? *(Chuckles.)*

ELLA: Very humorous.

WESTON: You want some breakfast? I was just fixin' something up for West, here.

ELLA: You're cooking?

WESTON: Yeah. What's it look like?

ELLA: Who did all this laundry?

WESTON: Yours truly.

ELLA: Are you having a nervous breakdown or what?

WESTON: Can't a man do his own laundry?

ELLA: As far as I know he can.

WESTON: Even did some a' yours too.

ELLA: Gee, thanks.

WESTON: Well, I coulda' just left it. I was doin' a load of my own, so I thought I'd throw everybody else's in to boot.

ELLA: I'm very grateful.

WESTON: So where you been. Off with that fancy lawyer?

ELLA: I've been to jail, like I said.

WESTON: Come on. What, on a visit? They throw you in the drunk tank? Out with it.

ELLA: I was visiting your daughter.

WESTON: O, yeah? What'd they nab her for?

ELLA: Possession of firearms. Malicious vandalism. Breaking and entering. Assault. Violation of equestrian regulations. You name it.

WESTON: Well, she always was a fireball.

ELLA: Part of the inheritance, right?

WESTON: Right. Direct descendant.

ELLA: Well, I'm glad you've found a way of turning shame into a source of pride.

WESTON: What's shameful about? Takes courage to get charged with all that stuff. It's not everyone her age who can run up a list of credits like that.

ELLA: That's for sure.

WESTON: Could you?

ELLA: Don't be ridiculous! I'm not self-destructive. Doesn't run in my family line.

WESTON: That's right. I never thought about it like that. You're the only one who doesn't have it. Only us.

ELLA: Oh, so now I'm the outsider.

WESTON: Well, it's true. You come from a different class of people. Gentle. Artists. They were all artists, weren't they?

ELLA: My grandfather was a pharmacist.

WESTON: Well, scientists then. Members of the professions. Professionals. Nobody raised their voice.

ELLA: That's bad?

WESTON: No. Just different. That's all. Just different.

ELLA: Are we waxing philosophical over our eggs now? Is that the idea? Sobered up over night, have we? Awoken to a brand-new morning? What is this crap! I've been down there all night trying to pull Emma back together again and I come back to Mr. Hyde! Mr. "Goody Two-Shoes"! Mister Mia Copa himself! Well, you can kiss off that crap because I'm not buying it!

WESTON: Would you like some coffee?

ELLA: NO. I DON'T WANT ANY GODDAMN COFEE! AND GET THAT SON-OF-A-BITCHING SHEEP OUT OF MY KITCHEN!!

WESTON: *(Staying cool.)* You've picked up on the lanaguage, okay, but your inflection's off.

ELLA: There's nothing wrong with my inflection!

WESTON: Something doesn't ring true about it. Something deep in the voice. At the heart of things.

ELLA: Oh, you are really something. How can you accuse me of not measuring up to your standards! You're a complete washout!

WESTON: It's got nothing to do with standards. It's more like fate.
ELLA: Oh, knock it off, would you? I'm exhausted.
WESTON: Try the table. Nice and hard. It'd do wonders for you.
ELLA: *(Suddenly soft.)* The table?
WESTON: Yeah. Just stretch yourself out. You'll be amazed. Better than any bed.

(Ella looks at the table for a second, then starts pushing all the clean laundry off it onto the floor. She pulls herself up onto it and stretches out on it. Weston goes on cooking with his back to her. She watches him as she lies there.)

WESTON: And when you wake up I'll have a great big breakfast of ham and eggs, ready and waiting. You'll feel like a million bucks. You'll wonder why you spent all those years in bed, once you feel that table. That table will deliver you.

(Wesley wanders onstage from stage left, completely naked, his hair wet. He looks dazed. Weston pays no attention but goes on preparing the breakfast and talking as Wesley wanders upstage and stares at Ella. She looks at him but doesn't react. He turns downstage and looks at Weston. He looks at the lamb and crosses down to it. He bends over and picks it up, then carries it off stage right. Weston goes on cooking and talking. Ella stays on the table.)

WESTON: That's the trouble with too much comfort, you know? Makes you forget where you come from. Makes you lose touch. You think you're making headway but you're losing all the time. You're falling behind more and more. You're going into a trance that you'll never come back from. You're being hypnotized. Your body's being mesmerized. You go into a coma. That's why you need a hard table once in a while to bring you back. A good hard table to bring you back to life.
ELLA: *(Still on table, sleepily.)* You should have been a preacher.
WESTON: You think so?
ELLA: Great voice you have. Deep. Resonates.

WESTON: *(Putting eggs on plate.)* I'm not a public person.

ELLA: I'm so exhausted.

WESTON: You just sleep.

ELLA: You should have seen that jail, Weston.

WESTON: I have.

ELLA: Oh, that's right. How could you ever sleep in a place like that?

WESTON: If you're numb enough you don't feel a thing. *(He yells off stage to Wesley.)* WES! YOUR BREAKFAST'S READY!

ELLA: He just went out.

WESTON: What?

ELLA: He just walked out stark naked with that sheep under his arm.

(Weston looks at fence enclosure, sees lamb gone. He's still holding plate.)

WESTON: Where'd he go?

ELLA: Outside.

WESTON: *(Crossing right, carrying plate.)* WES! GODDAMNIT, YOUR BREAKFAST'S READY!

(Weston exits carrying plate off stage right. Ella tries to keep her eyes open, still on table.)

ELLA: *(To herself.)* Nothing surprises me anymore.

(She slowly falls asleep on table. Nothing happens for a while. Then Weston comes back on from right still carrying plate. Ella stays asleep on table.)

WESTON: *(Crossing to stove.)* He's not out there. Wouldn't ya' know it? Just when it's ready, he walks out. *(Turning to Ella.)* Why'd he take the lamb? That lamb needs to be kept warm. *(Sees that Ella's sound asleep.)* Great. *(Turns and sets plate down on stove; looks at food.)* Might as well eat it myself. A double breakfast. Why not? *(He starts eating of the plate, talks to himself.)* Can't expect the thing to get well if it's not kept warm. *(He turns upstage again and looks at Ella sleeping, then turns back to the plate of food.)* Always was best at talkin' to myself. Always was the best thing. Nothing like it. Keeps ya' company at least.

(Wesley enters from right dressed in Weston's baseball cap, overcoat, and tennis shoes. He stands there. Weston looks at him. Ella sleeps.)

WESTON: What in the hell's goin' on with you? I was yellin' for you just now. Didn't you hear me?

WESLEY: *(Staring at Weston.)* No.

WESTON: Your breakfast was all ready. Now it's cold. I've eaten half of it already. Almost half gone.

WESLEY: *(Blankly.)* You can have it.

WESTON: What're you doin' in those clothes anyway?

WESLEY: I found them.

WESTON: I threw them out! What's got into you? You go take a bath and then put on some old bum's clothes that've been thrown-up in, pissed in, and God knows what all in?

WESLEY: They fit me.

WESTON: I can't fathom you, that's for sure. What'd you do with that lamb?

WESLEY: Butchered it.

WESTON: *(Turning away from him, disgusted.)* I swear to God. *(Pause, then turning to Wesley.)* WHAT'D YA' BUTCHER THE DUMB THING FOR!

WESLEY: We need some food.

WESTON: THE ICE BOX IS CRAMMED FULL A' FOOD!

(Wesley crosses quickly to refrigerator, opens it, and starts pulling all kinds of food out and eating it ravenously. Weston watches him, a little afraid of Wesley's state.)

WESTON: WHAT'D YA' GO AND BUTCHER IT FOR? HE WAS GETTING BETTER! *(Watches Wesley eating hungrily.)* What's a' matter with you, boy? I made ya' a big breakfast. Why didn't ya' eat that? What's the matter with you?

(Weston moves cautiously, away from Wesley to stage right. Wesley keeps eating, throwing half-eaten food to one side and then digging into more. He groans slightly as he eats.)

WESTON: *(To Wesley.)* Look, I know I ignored some a' the chores around the place and you had to do it instead a' me. But I brought you some artichokes back, didn't I? Didn't I do that? I didn't have to do that. I went outa' my way. I saw the sign on the highway and drove two miles outa' my way just to bring you back some artichokes. *(Pause, as he looks at Wesley eating; he glances nervously up at Ella, then back to Wesley.)* You couldn't be all that starving! We're not that bad off, goddamnit! I've seen starving people in my time, and we're not that bad off! *(Pause, no reaction from Wesley, who continues to eat ravenously.)* You just been spoiled, that's all! This is a paradise for a young person! There's kids your age who'd give their eyeteeth to have an environment like this to grow up in! You've got everything! Everything! Opportunity is glaring you in the teeth here! *(Turns toward Ella.)* ELLA! ELLA, WAKE UP! *(No reaction from Ella; turns back to Wesley, still eating.)* If this is supposed to make me feel guilty, it's not working! It's not working because I don't have to pay for my past now! Not now! Not after this morning! All that's behind me now! YOU UNDERSTAND ME? IT'S ALL OVER WITH BECAUSE I'VE BEEN REBORN! I'M A WHOLE NEW PERSON NOW! I'm a whole new person.

(Wesley stops eating suddenly and turns to Weston.)

WESLEY: *(Coldly.)* They're going to kill you.

WESTON: *(Pause.)* Who's going to kill me! What're you talking about! Nobody's going to kill me!

WESLEY: I couldn't get the money.

WESTON: What money?

WESLEY: Ellis.

WESTON: So what?

WESLEY: You owe it to them.

WESTON: Owe it to who? I don't remember anything. All that's over with now.

WESLEY: No, it's not. It's still there. Maybe you've changed, but you still owe them.

WESTON: I can't remember. Must've borrowed some for the car payment. Can't remember it.

WESLEY: They remember it.

WESTON: So, I'll get it to them. It's not that drastic.

WESLEY: How? Ellis has the house and everything now.

WESTON: How does he have the house? This is my house!

WESLEY: You signed it over.

WESTON: I never signed anything!

WESLEY: You were drunk.

WESTON: SHUT UP!

WESLEY: How're you going to pay them?

WESTON: *(Pause.)* I can sell that land.

WESLEY: It's phony land. The guy's run off to Mexico.

WESTON: What guy?

WESLEY: Taylor. The lawyer. The lawyer friend of Mom's.

WESTON: *(Pause, looks at Ella sleeping, then back to Wesley.)* Same guy?

WESLEY: Same guy. Ripped us all off.

WESTON: This isn't right. I was on a whole new track. I was getting right up on top of it all.

WESLEY: They've got it worked out so you can't.

WESTON: I was ready for a whole new attack. This isn't right!

WESLEY: They've moved in on us like a creeping disease. We didn't even notice.

WESTON: I just built a whole new door and everything. I washed all the laundry. I cleaned up all the artichokes. I started over.

WESLEY: You better run.

WESTON: Run? What do you mean, run? I can't run!

WESLEY: Take the Packard and get out of here.

WESTON: I can't run out on everything.

WESLEY: Why not?

WESTON: 'CAUSE THIS IS WHERE I SETTLED DOWN! THIS IS WHERE THE LINE ENDED! RIGHT HERE! I MIGRATED TO THIS SPOT! I GOT NOWHERE TO GO TO! THIS IS IT!

WESLEY: Take the Packard.

(Weston stands there for a while. He looks around, trying to figure a way out.)

WESTON: *(After pause.)* I remember now. I was in hock. I was in hock up to my elbows. See, I always figured on the future. I banked on it. I was banking on it getting better. It couldn't get worse, so I figured it'd just get better. I figured that's why everyone wants you to buy things. Buy refrigerators. Buy cars, houses, lots, invest. They wouldn't be so generous if they didn't figure you had it comin' in. At some point it had to be comin' in. So I went along with it. Why not borrow if you know it's coming in. Why not make a touch here and there. They all want you to borrow anyhow. Banks, car lots, investors. The whole thing's geared to invisible money. You never hear the sound of change anymore. It's all plastic shuffling back and forth. It's all in everybody's heads. So I figured if that's the case, why not take advantage of it? Why not go in debt for a few grand if all it is is numbers? If it's all an idea and nothing's really there, why not take advantage? So I just went along with it, that's all. I just played ball.

WESLEY: You better go.

(Pause, as Weston looks at Ella sleeping.)

WESTON: Same guy, huh? She musta' known about it, too. She musta' thought I left her.

(Weston turns and looks at Wesley. Silence.)

WESLEY: You did.

WESTON: I just went off for a little while. Now and then. I couldn't stand it here. I couldn't stand the idea that everything would stay the same. That every morning it would be the same. I kept looking for it out there somewhere. I kept trying to piece it together. The jumps. I couldn't figure out the jumps. From being born, to growing up, to droppin' bombs, to having kids, to hittin' bars, to this. It all turned on me somehow. It all turned around on me. I kept looking for it out there somewhere. And all the time it was right inside this house.

WESLEY: They'll be coming for you here. They know where you live now.

WESTON: Where should I go?

WESLEY: How 'bout Mexico?

WESTON: Mexico? Yeah. That's where everyone escapes to, right? It's full of escape artists down there. I could go down there and get lost. I could disappear. I could start a whole new life down there.

WESLEY: Maybe.

WESTON: I could find that guy and get my money back. That real estate guy. What's his name?

WESLEY: Taylor.

WESTON: Yeah, Taylor. He'd down there too, right? I could find him.

WESLEY: Maybe.

WESTON: *(Looking over at Ella again.)* I can't believe she knew and still went off with him. She musta' thought I was dead or something. She musta' thought I was never coming back.

(Weston moves toward Ella, then stops. He looks at Wesley, then turns and exits off right. Wesley just stands there. Wesley bends down and picks some scraps of food up off the floor and eats them very slowly. He looks at the empty lamb pen . . .)

****

from **BURIED CHILD** (1978)
Act Three

CHARACTERS

Shelly
Dewis
Halie
Bradley
Dodge
Vince
Tilden

[In this excerpt, Dodge, the infirm and dying father, is propped against the television. His son Bradley, who is physically handicapped, lies on the couch he has usurped from Dodge along with his father's blanket. The mentally burned-out Tilden has disappeared into the backyard. Halie, the disassociated mother, has returned to the house she left the day before with Father Dewis, the hypocritical and ineffective priest. Shelly, the outsider and "witness" character, has been abandoned in the house by Vince, her boyfriend and Dodge's grandson, and victimized and terrified by Dodge and Bradley. She has finally had enough and grabs Bradley's wooden leg, holding it like a weapon.]

SHELLY: Don't come near me! Don't anyone come near me. I don't need any words from you. I'm not threatening anybody. I don't even know what I'm doing here. You all say you don't remember Vince, okay, maybe you don't. Maybe it's Vince that's crazy. Maybe he's made this whole family thing up. I don't even care anymore. I was just coming along for the ride. I thought it'd be a nice geature. Besides, I was curious. He made all of you sound familiar to me. Every one of you. For every name, I had an image. Every time he'd tell me a name, I'd see the person. In fact, each of you was so clear in my mind that I actually believed it was you. I really believed when I walked through that door that the people who lived here would turn out to be the same people in my imagination. But I don't recognize any of you. Not one. Not even the slightest resemblance.

DEWIS: Well you can hardly blame others for not fulfilling your hallucination.

SHELLY: It was no hallucination! It was more like a prophecy. You believe in prophecy, don't you?

HALIE: Father, there's no point in talking to her any further. We're just going to have to call the police.

BRADLEY: No! Don't get the police in here. We don't want the police in here. This is our home.

SHELLY: That's right. Bradley's right. Don't you usually settle your affairs in private? Don't you usually take them out in the dark? Out in the back?

BRADLEY: You stay out of our lives! You have no business interfering!

SHELLY: I don't have any business period. I got nothing to lose.

(She moves around, staring at each of them.)

BRADLEY: You don't know what we've been through. You don't know anything!

SHELLY: I know you've got a secret. You've all got a secret. It's so secret in fact, you're all convinced it never happened.

(Halie moved to Dewis.)

HALIE: O, my God, Father!

DODGE: *(Laughing to himself.)* She thinks she's going to get it out of us. She thinks she's going to uncover the truth of the matter. Like a detective or something.

BRADLEY: I'm not telling her anything! Nothing's wrong here! Nothing's ever been wrong! Everything's the way it's supposed to be! Nothing ever happened that's bad! Everything is all right here! We're all good people!

DODGE: She thinks she's gonna suddenly bring everything out into the open after all these years.

DEWIS: *(To Shelly.)*: Can't you see these people want to be left in peace? Don't you have any mercy? They haven't done anything to you.

DODGE: She wants to get to the bottom of it. *(To Shelly.)* That's it, isn't it? You'd like to get right down to bedrock? You want me to tell ya'? You want me to tell ya' what happened? I'l tell ya'. I might as well.

BRADLEY: No! Don't listen to him. He doesn't remember anything!

DODGE: I remember the whole thing from start to finish. I remember the day he was born.

(Pause.)

HALIE: Dodge, if you tell this thing — if you tell this, you'll be dead to me. You'll be just as good as dead.

DODGE: That won't be such a big change, Halie. See this girl, this girl here, she wants to know. She wants to know something more. And I got this feeling that it doesn't make a bit a' difference. I'd sooner tell it to a stranger than anybody else.

BRADLEY: *(To Dodge.)* We made a pact! We made a pact between us! You can't break that now!

DODGE: I don't remember any pact.

BRADLEY: *(To Shelly.)* See, he doesn't remember anything. I'm the only one in the family who remembers. The only one. And I'll never tell you!

SHELLY: I'm not so sure I want to find out now.

DODGE: *(Laughing to himself.)* Listen to her! Now she's runnin' scared!

SHELLY: I'm not scared!

(Dodge stops laughing, long pause. Dodge stares at her.)

DODGE: You're not hugh? Well, that's good. Because I'm not either. See, we were a well established family once. Well established. All the boys were grown. The farm was producing enough milk to fill Lake Michigan twice over. Me and Halie here were pointed toward what looked like the middle part of our life. Everything was settled with us. All we had to do was ride it out. Then Halie got pregnant again. Outa' the middle a' nowhere, she got pregnant. We weren't planning on havin' any more boys. We had enough boys already. In fact, we hadn't been sleepin' in the same bed for about six years.

HALIE: *(Moving toward stairs.)* I'm not listening to this! I don't have to listen to this!

DODGE: *(Stops Halie.)* Where are you going! Upstairs! You'll just be listenin' to it upstairs! You go outside, you'll be listenin' to it outside. Might as well stay here and listen to it.

(Halie stays by stairs.)

BRADLEY: If I had my leg you wouldn't be saying this. You'd never get away with it if I had my leg.

DODGE: *(Pointing to Shelly.)* She's got your leg. *(Laughs.)* She's gonna keep your leg too. *(To Shelly.)* She wants to hear this. Don't you?

SHELLY: I don't know.

DODGE: Well even if ya' don't I'm gonna' tell ya'. *(Pause.)* Halie had this kid. This baby boy. She had it. I let her have it on her own. All the other boys I had had the best doctors, best nurses, everything. This one I let her have by herself. This one hurt real bad. Almost killed her, but she had it anyway. It lived, see. It lived. It wanted to grow up in this family. It wanted to be just like us. It wanted to be a part of us. It wanted to pretend that I was its father. She wanted me to believe in it. Even when everyone around us knew. Everyone. All our boys knew. Tilden knew.

HALIE: You shut up! Bradley, make him shut up!

BRADLEY: I can't.

DODGE: Tilden was the one who knew. Better than any of us. He'd walk for miles with that kid in his arms. Halie let him take it. All night sometimes. He'd walk all night out there in the pasture with it. Talkin' to it. Singin' to it. Used to hear him singing to it. He'd make up stories. He'd tell that kid all kinds a' stories. Even when he knew it couldn't understand. Couldn't understand a word he was sayin'. Never would understand him. We couldn't let a thing like that continue. We couldn't allow that to grow up right in the middle of our lives. It made everything we'd accomplished look like it was nothin'. Everything was cancelled out by this one mistake. This one weakness.

SHELLY: So you killed him?

DODGE: I killed it. I drowned it. Just like the runt of a litter. Just drowned it.

(Halie moves toward Bradley.)

HALIE: *(To Bradley.)* Ansel wouldn've stopped him! Ansel would've stopped him from telling these lies! He was a hero! A man! A whole man! What's happened to the men in this family! Where are the men!

(Suddenly Vince comes crashing through the screen porch door up left, tearing it off its hinges. Everyone but Dodge and Bradley back away from the porch and stare at Vince who has landed on his stomach on the porch in a drunken stupor. He is singing loudly to himself and hauls himself slowly to his feet. He has a paper shopping bag full of empty booze bottles. He takes them out one at a time as he sings and smashes them at the opposite end of the porch, behind the solid interior door, stage right. Shelly moves slowly toward stage right, holding wooden leg and watching Vince.)

VINCE: *(Singing loudly as he hurls bottles.)* "From the Halls of Montezuma to the Shores of Tripoli. We will fight our country's battles on the land and on the sea."

(He punctuates the words "Montezuma," "Tripoli," "battles," and "sea" with a smashed battle each. He stops throwing for a second, stares toward stage right of the porch, shades his eyes with his hand as though looking across to a battle field, then cups his hands around his mouth and yells across the space of the porch to an imaginary army. The others watch in terror and expectation.)

VINCE: *(To imagined army.)* Have you had enough over there! 'Cause there's a lot more here where that came from! *(Pointing to paper bag full of bottles.)* A helluva lot more! We got enough over here to blow ya' from here to Kingdomcome!

(He takes another bottle, makes high whistling sound of a bomb and throws it toward stage right porch. Sound of bottle smashing against wall. This should be the actual smashing of bottles and not tape sound. He keeps yelling and heaving bottles one after another. Vince stops for a while, breathing heavily from exhaustion. Long silence as the others watch him. Shelly approaches tentatively in Vince's direction, still holding Bradley's wooden leg.)

SHELLY: *(After silence.)* Vince?

(Vince turns toward her. Peers through screen.)

VINCE: Who? What? Vince who? Who's that in there?

(Vince pushes his face against the screen from the porch and stares in at everyone.)

DODGE: Where's my goddamn bottle!
VINCE: *(Looking in at Dodge.)* What? Who is that?
DODGE: It's me! Your Grandfather! Don't play stupid with me! Where's my two bucks!
VINCE: Your two bucks?

(Halie moves away from Dewis, upstage, peers out at Vince, trying to recognize him.)

HALIE: Vincent? Is that you, Vincent?

(Shelly stares at Halie then looks out at Vince.)

VINCE: *(From porch.)* Vincent who? What is this! Who are you people?
SHELLY: *(To Halie.)* Hey, wait a minute. Wait a minute! What's going on?

HALIE: *(Moving closer to porch screen.)* We thought you were a murderer or something. Barging in through the door like that.

VINCE: I am a murderer! Don't underestimate me for a minute! I'm the Midnight Strangler! I devour whole families in a single gulp!

(Vince grabs another bottle and smashes it on the porch. Halie backs away.)

SHELLY: *(Approaching Halie.)* You mean you know who he is?

HALIE: Of course I know who he is! That's more than I can say for you.

BRADLEY: *(Sitting up on sofa.)* You get off our front porch you creep! What're you doing out there breaking bottles? Who are these foreigners anyway! Where did they come from?

VINCE: Maybe I should come in there and break them!

HALIE: *(Moving toward porch.)* Don't you dare! Vincent, what's got into you! Why are you acting like this?

VINCE: Maybe I should come in there and usurp your territory!

(Halie turns back toward Dewis and crosses to him.)

HALIE: *(To Dewis.)* Father, why are you just standing around here when everything's falling apart? Can't you rectify this situation?

(Dodge laughs, coughs.)

DEWIS: I'm just a guest here, Halie. I don't know what my position is exactly. This is outside my parish anyway.

(Vince starts throwing more bottles as things continue.)

BRADLEY: If I had my leg I'd rectify it! I'd rectify him all over the goddamn highway! I'd pull his ears out if I could reach him!

(Bradley sticks his fist through the screening of the porch and reaches out for Vince jumps away from Bradley's hand.)

VINCE: Aaaah! Our lines have been penetrated! Tentacled animals! Beasts from the deep!

(Vince strikes out at Bradley's hand with a bottle. Bradley pulls his hand back inside.)

SHELLY: Vince! Knock it off will ya'! I want to get out of here!

(Vince pushes his face against screen, looks in at Shelly.)

VINCE: *(To Shelly.)* Have they got you prisoner in there, dear? Such a sweet young thing too. All her life in front of her. Nipped in the bud.

SHELLY: I'm coming out there, Vince! I'm coming out there and I want us to get in the car and rive away from here. Anywhere. Just away from here.

(Shelly moves toward Vince's saxophone case and overcoat. She sets down the wooden leg, downstage left and picks up the saxophone case and overcoat. Vince watches her through the screen.)

VINCE: *(To Shelly.)* We'll have to negotiate. Make some kind of a deal. Prisoner exchange or something. A few of theirs for one of ours. Small price to pay if you ask me.

(Shelly crosses toward stage right door with overcoat and case.)

SHELLY: Just go and get the car! I'm coming out there now. We're going to leave.

VINCE: Don't come out here! Don't you dare come out here!

(Shelly stops short of the door, stage right.)

SHELLY: How come?

VINCE: Off limits! Verboten! This is taboo territory. No man or woman has ever crossed the line and lived to tell the tale!

SHELLY: I'll take my chances.

(Shelly moves to stage right door and opens it. Vince pulls out a big folding hunting knife and pulls open the blade. He jabs the blade into the screen and starts cutting a hole big enough to climb through. Bradley cowers in a corner of the sofa as Vince rips at the screen.)

VINCE: *(As he cuts screen.)* Don't come out here! I'm warning you! You'll disintegrate!

(Dewis takes Halie by the arm and pulls her toward staircase.)

DEWIS: Halie, maybe we should go upstairs until this blows over.

HALIE: I don't understand it. I just don't understand it. He was the sweetest little boy!

(Dewis drops the roses beside the wooden leg at the foot of the staircase then escorts Halie quickly up the stairs. Halie keeps looking back at Vince as they climb the stairs.)

HALIE: There wasn't a mean bone in his body. Everyone loved Vincent. Everyone. He was the perfect baby.

DEWIS: He'll be all right after a while. He's just had a few too many that's all.

HALIE: He used to sing in his sleep. He'd sing. In the middle of the night. The sweetest voice. Like an angel. *(She stops for a moment.)* I used to lie awake listening to it. I used to lie awake thinking it was all right if I died. Because Vincent was an angel. A guardian angel. He'd watch over us. He'd watch over all of us.

(Dewis takes her all the way up the stairs. They disappear above. Vince is now climbing through the porch screen onto the sofa. Bradley crashes off the sofa, holding tight to his blanket, keeping it wrapped around him. Shelly is outside on the porch. Vince holds the knife in his teeth once he gets the hole wide enough to climb through. Bradley starts crawling slowly toward his wooden leg, reaching out for it.)

DODGE: *(To Vince.)* Go ahead! Take over the house! Take over the whole goddamn house! You can have it! It's yours. It's been a pain in the neck ever since the very first mortgage. I'm gonna die any second now. Any second. You won't even notice. So I'll settle my affairs once and for all.

(As Dodge proclaims his last will and testament, Vince climbs into the room, knife in mouth, and strides slowly around the space, inspecting his inheritance. He casually notices Bradley as he crawls toward his leg. Vince moves to the leg and keeps pushing it with his foot so that it's out of Bradley's reach then goes on with his inspection. He picks up the roses and carries them around smelling them. Shelly can be seen outside on the porch, moving slowly center and staring in at Vince. Vince ignores her.)

DODGE: The house goes to my Grandson, Vincent. All the furnishings, accoutrements and paraphernalia therein. Everything tacked to the walls or otherwise resting under this roof. My tools — namely my band saw, my skill saw, my drill press, my chain saw, my lathe, my electric sander, all go to my eldest son, Tilden. That is, if he ever shows up again. My shed and gasoline powered equipment, namely my tractor, my dozer, my hand tiller plus all the attachments and riggings for the above mentioned machinery, namely my spring tooth harrow, my deep plows, my disk plows, my automatic fertilizing equipment, my reaper, my swathe, my seeder, my John Deere Harvester, my post hole digger, my jackhammer, my lath — *(To himself.)* Did I mention my lathe? I already mentioned my lathe — my Bennie Goodman records, my harnesses, my bits, my halters, my brace, my rough rasp, my forge, my welding equipment, my shoeing nails, my levels and bevels, my milking stool — no, not my milking stool — my hammers and chisels, my hinges, my cattle gates, my barbed wire, self-tapping augers, my horse hair ropes and all related materials are to be pushed into a gigantic heap and set ablaze in the very center of my fields. When the blaze is at its highest, preferably on a cold, windless night, my body is to be pitched into the middle of it and burned til nothing remains but ash.

(Pause. Vince takes the knife out of his mouth and smells the roses. He's facing toward audience and doesn't turn around to Shelly. He folds up knife and pockets it.)

SHELLY: *(From porch.)* I'm leaving, Vince. Whether you come or not, I'm leaving.

VINCE: *(Smelling roses.)* Just put my horn on the couch there before you take off.

SHELLY: *(Moving toward hole in screen.)* You're not coming?

(Vince stays downstage, turns and looks at her.)

VINCE: I just inherited a house.

SHELLY: *(Through hole, from porch.)* You want to stay here?

VINCE: *(as he pushes Bradley's leg out of reach)* I've gotta carry on the line. I've gotta see to it that things keep rolling.

(Bradley looks up at him from floor, keeps pulling himself toward his leg. Vince keeps moving it.)

SHELLY: What happened to you, Vince? You just disappeared.

VINCE: *(Pause, delivers speech front.)* I was gonna run last night. I was gonna run and keep right on running. I drove all night. Clear to the Iowa border. The old man's two bucks sitting right on the seat beside me. It never stopped raining the whole time. Never stopped once. I could see myself in the windshield. My face. My eyes. I studied my face. Studied everything about it. As though I was looking at another man. As though I could see his whole race behind him. Like a mummy's face. I saw him dead and alive at the same time. In the same breath. In the windshield, I watched him breathe as though he was frozen in time. And every breath marked him. Marked him forever without him knowing. And then his face changed. His face became his father's face. Same bones. Same eyes. Same nose. Same breath. And his father's face changed to his Grandfather's face. And it went on like that. Changing. Clear on back to faces I'd never seen before but still recognized. Still recognized the bones underneath. The eyes. The breath. The mouth. I followed my family clear into Iowa. Every last one. Straight into the Corn Belt and further. Straight back as far as they'd take me. Then it all dissolved. Everything dissolved.

(Shelly stares at him for a while then reaches through the hole in the screen and sets the saxophone case and Vince's overcoat on the sofa. She looks at Vince again.)

SHELLY: Bye Vince.

(She exits off the porch. Vince watches her go. Bradley tries to make a lunge for his wooden leg. Vince quickly picks it up and dangles it over Bradle's head like a carrot. Bradley keeps making desperate grabs at the leg. Dewis comes down the staircase and stops halfway, staring at Vince and Bradley. Vince looks up at Dewis and smiles. He keeps moving backwards with the leg toward upstage left as Bradley crawls after him.)

VINCE: *(To Dewis as he continues torturing Bradley.)* Oh, excuse me Father. Just getting rid of some of the vermin in the house. This is my house now, ya' know? All mine. Everything. Except for the power tools and stuff. I'm gonna get all new equipment anyway. New plows, new tractor, everything. All brand new. *(Vince teases Bradley closer to the up left corner of the stage.)* Start right off on the ground floor.

(Vince throws Bradley's wooden leg far off stage left. Bradley follows his leg off stage, pulling himself along on the ground, whimpering. As Bradley exits Vince pulls the blanket off him and throws it over his own shoulder. He crosses toward Dewis with the blanket and smells the roses. Dewis comes to the bottom of the stairs.)

DEWIS: You'd better go up and see your Grandmother.

VINCE: *(Looking up stairs, back to Dewis.)* My grandmother? There's nobody else in this house. Except for you. And you're leaving aren't you?

(Dewis crosses toward stage right door. He turns back to Vince.)

DEWIS: She's going to need someone. I can't help her. I don't know what to do. I don't know what my position is. I just came in for some tea. I had no idea there was any trouble. No idea at all.

(Vince just stares at him. Dewis goes out the door, crosses porch and exits left. Vince listens to him leaving. He smells roses, looks up the staircase then smells roses again. He turns and looks upstage at Dodge. He crosses up to him and bends over looking at Dodge's open eyes. Dodge is dead. His death should have come completely unnoticed. Vince lifts the blanket, then covers his head. He sits on the sofa, smelling roses and staring at Dodge's body. Long pause. Vince places the roses on Dodge's chest then lays down on the sofa, arms folded behind his head, staring at the ceiling. His body is in the same relationship to Dodge's. After a while Halie's voice is heard coming from above the staircase. The lights start to dim almost imperceptibly as Halie speaks. Vince keeps staring at the ceiling)

HALIE'S VOICE: Dodge? Is that you Dodge? Tilden was right about the corn you know. I've never seen such corn. Have you taken a look at it lately? Tall as a man already. This early in the year. Carrots too. Potatoes. Peas. It's like a paradise over there, Dodge. You oughta' take a look. A miracle. I've never seen it like this. Maybe the rain did something. Maybe it was the rain.

(As Halie keeps talking off stage, Tilden appears from stage left, dripping with mud from the knees down. His arms and hands are covered with mud. In his hands he carries the corpse of a small child at chest level, staring down at it. The corpse mainly consists of bones wrapped in muddy, rotten cloth. He moves slowly downstage toward the staircase, ignoring Vince on the sofa. Vince keeps staring at the ceiling as though Tilden wasn't there. As Halie's voice continues, Tilden slowly makes his way up the stairs. His eyes never leave the corpse of the child. The lights keep fading.)

HALIE'S VOICE: Good hard rain. Takes everything straight down deep to the roots. The rest takes care of itself. You can't force a thing to grow. You can't interfere with it. It's all hidden. It's all unseen. You just gotta wait til it pops up out of the ground. Tiny little shoot. Tiny little white shoot. All hairy and fragile. Strong though. Strong enough to break the earth even. It's a miracle, Dodge. I've never seen a crop like this in my whole life. Maybe it's the sun. Maybe that's it. Maybe it's the sun.

(Tilden disappears above. Silence. Lights go to black.)

****

from **TRUE WEST** (1980)
Scene 7

CHARACTERS

Lee
Austin

[This play, written in nine scenes, displays many of the themes that run through Shepard's canon. In *True West*, the relationship between the hostile, dominating father and the son who attempts reconciliation is replaced by the battle between brothers Lee and Austin.

The play examines the reality versus the myth of the true West. In a Shepardesque "aria," a term frequently used to describe Shepard's long, imagistic monologues, Austin describes a visit with his father that obliterated the romantic image of the Hollywood West, replacing it with the true West.]

LEE: Just hang on a minute, Austin.

AUSTIN: Why? What for? You don't need my help, right? You got a handle on the project. Besides, I'm lookin' forward to the smell of the night. The bushes. Orange blossoms. Dust in the driveways. Rain bird sprinklers. Lights in people's houses. You're right about the lights, Lee. Everybody else is livin' the life. Indoors. Safe. This is a Paradise down here. You know that? We're livin' in a Paradise. We've forgotten about that.

LEE: You sound just like the old man now.

AUSTIN: Yeah, well we all sound alike when we're sloshed. We just sorta echo each other.

LEE: Maybe if we could work on this together we could bring him back out here. Get him settled down some place.

(Austin turns violently toward Lee, takes a swing at him, misses and crashes to the floor again. Lee stays standing.)

AUSTIN: I don't want him out here! I've had it with him! I went all the way out there! I went out of my way. I gave him money and all he did was play Al Jolson records and spit at me! I gave him money!

(Pause.)

LEE: Just help me a little with the characters, all right? You know how to do it, Austin.

AUSTIN: *(On floor, laughs.)* The characters!

LEE: Yeah. You know. The way they talk and stuff. I can hear it in my head but I can't get it down on paper.

AUSTIN: What characters?

LEE: The guys. The guys in the story.

AUSTIN: Those aren't characters.

LEE: Whatever you call 'em then. I need to write somethin' out.

AUSTIN: Those are illusions of characters.

LEE: I don't give a damn what ya' call 'em! You know what I'm talkin' about!

AUSTIN: Those are fantasies of a long lost boyhood.

LEE: I gotta' write somethin' out on paper!!

(Pause.)

AUSTIN: What for? Saul's gonna' get you a fancy screenwriter isn't he?

LEE: I wanna' do it myself!

AUSTIN: Then do it! Yer on your own now, old buddy. You bulldogged yer way into contention. Now you gotta' carry it through.

LEE: I will but I need some advice. Just a couple a' things. Come on, Austin. Just help me get 'em talkin' right. It won't take much.

AUSTIN: Oh, now you're having a little doubt huh? What happened? The pressure's on, boy. This is it. You gotta' come up with it now.

You don't come up with a winner on your first time out they just cut your head off. They don't give you a second chance ya' know.

LEE: I got a good story! I know it's a good story. I just need a little help is all.

AUSTIN: Not from me. Not from yer little old brother. I'm retired.

LEE: You could save this thing for me, Austin. I'd give ya' half the money. I would. I only need half anyway. With this kinda' money I could be a long time down the road. I'd never bother ya' again. I promise. You'd never even see me again.

AUSTIN: *(Still on floor.)* You'd disappear?

LEE: I would for sure.

AUSTIN: Where would you disappear to?

LEE: That don't matter. I got plenty a' places.

AUSTIN: Nobody can disappear. The old man tried that. Look where it got him. He lost his teeth.

LEE: He never had any money.

AUSTIN: I don't mean that. I mean his teeth! His real teeth. First he lost his real teeth, then he lost his false teeth. You never knew that did ya'? He never confided in you.

LEE: Nah, I never knew that.

AUSTIN: You wanna drink?

(Austin offers bottle to Lee, Lee takes it, sits down on kitchen floor with Austin, they share the bottle.)

AUSTIN: Yeah, he lost his real teeth one at a time. Woke up every morning with another tooth lying on the mattress. Finally, he decides he's gotta get 'em all pulled out but he doesn't have any money. Middle of Arizona with no money and no insurance and every morning another tooth is lying on the mattress. *(Takes a drink.)* So what does he do?

LEE: I dunno. I never knew about that.

AUSTIN: He begs the government. G.I. Bill or some damn thing. Some pension plan he remembers in the back of his head. And they send him out the money.

LEE: They did?

(They keep trading the bottle between them, taking drinks.)

AUSTIN: Yeah. They send him the money but it's not enough money. Costs a lot to have all yer teeth yanked. They charge by the individual tooth, ya know. I mean one tooth isn't equal to another tooth. Some are more expensive. Like the big ones in the back —

LEE: So what happened?

AUSTIN: So he locates a Mexican dentist in Juarez who'll do the whole thing for a song. And he takes off hitchhiking to the border.

LEE: Hitchhiking?

AUSTIN: Yeah. So how long you think it takes him to get to the border? A man his age.

LEE: I dunno.

AUSTIN: Eight days it takes him. Eight days in the rain and the sun and every day he's droppin' teeth on the black top and nobody'll pick him up 'cause his mouth's full a' blood.

(Pause, they drink.)

AUSTIN: So finally he stumbles into the dentist. Dentist takes all his money and all his teeth. And there he is, in Mexico, with his gums sewed up and his pockets empty.

(Long silence, Austin drinks.)

LEE: That's it?

AUSTIN: Then I go out to see him. See. I go out there and I take him out for a nice Chinese dinner. But he doesn't eat. All he wants to do is drink Martinis outa' plastic cups. And he takes his teeth out and lays 'em on the table 'cause he can't stand the feel of 'em. And we ask the waitress for one a' those doggie bags to take the Chop Suey home in. So he drops his teeth in the doggie bag along with the Chop Suey. And then we go out to hit all the bars up and down the highway. Says he wants to introduce me to all his buddies. And in one a' those bars, in one a' those bars up and down the highway, he left that doggie bag with his teeth laying in the Chop Suey.

LEE: You never found it?

AUSTIN: We went back but we never did find it. *(Pause.)* Now that's a true story. True to life.

(They drink as lights fade to black.)

****

from FOOL FOR LOVE (1983)

CHARACTERS

Martin
Eddie
The Old Man
May

[The play takes place in a "Stark, low-rent motel room on the edge of the Mojave Desert." May has left the mobile home she and Eddie shared after Eddie, a Hollywood stuntman, deserted her for a starlet. We learn as the play unfolds that this is a repeated pattern in their relationship as the couple continue to reunite, and Eddie inevitably and repeatedly deserts May. The Old Man sits in the rocker facing up right so that he's just slightly in profile to the audience. He is the "ghost" of the father.

In this excerpt, Eddie confronts Martin, the character who functions as a witness to the confessions of the other characters. He has come to pick May up for a date, but May has fled to the bathroom to avoid the confrontation.]

MARTIN: And you're not really cousins?
EDDIE: No. Not really. No.
MARTIN: You're — her husband?
EDDIE: No. She's my sister. *(He and The Old Man look at each other, then he turns back to Martin.)* My half-sister.

(Pause. Eddie and The Old Man drink.)

MARTIN: Your sister?
EDDIE: Yeah.
MARTIN: Oh. So — you knew each other even before high school then, huh?

EDDIE: No, see, I never even knew I had a sister until it was too late.

MARTIN: How do you mean?

EDDIE: Well, by the time I found out we'd already — you know — fooled around.

(The old man shakes his head, drinks. Long pause. Martin just stares at Eddie.)

EDDIE: *(Grins.)* Whatsa' matter, Martin?

MARTIN: You fooled around?

EDDIE: Yeah.

MARTIN: Well — um — that's illegal, isn't it?

EDDIE: I suppose so.

THE OLD MAN: *(To Eddie.)* Who is this guy?

MARTIN: I mean — is that true? She's really your sister?

EDDIE: Half. Only half.

MARTIN: Which half?

EDDIE: Top half. In horses we call that the "topside."

THE OLD MAN: Yeah, and the mare's what? The mare's uh — "distaff," isn't it? Isn't that the bottom half? "Distaff." Funny I should remember that.

MARTIN: And you fooled around in high school together?

EDDIE: Yeah. Sure. Everybody fooled around in high school. Didn't you?

MARTIN: No. I never did.

EDDIE: Maybe you should have, Martin.

MARTIN: Well, not with my sister.

EDDIE: No, I wouldn't recommend that.

MARTIN: How could that happen? I mean —

EDDIE: Well, see — *(Pause, he stares at The Old Man.)* — our daddy fell in love twice. That's basically how it happened. Once with my mother and once with her mother.

THE OLD MAN: I was the same love. Just got split in two, that's all.

MARTIN: Well, how come you didn't know each other until high school, then?

EDDIE: He had two separate lives. That's how come. Two completely separate lives. He'd live with me and my mother for a while and then he's disappear and go live with her and her mother for a while.

THE OLD MAN: Now don't be too hard on me, boy. It can happen to the best of us.

MARTIN: And you never knew what was going on?

EDDIE: Nope. Neither did my mother.

THE OLD MAN: She knew.

EDDIE: *(To Martin.)* She never knew.

MARTIN: She must've suspected something was going on.

EDDIE: Well, if she did she never let on to me. Maybe she was afraid of finding out. Or maybe she just loved him. I don't know. He'd disappear for months at a time and she never once asked him where he went. She was always glad to see him when he came back. The two of us used to go running out of the house to meet him as soon as we saw the Studebaker coming across the field.

THE OLD MAN: *(To Eddie.)* That was no Studebaker, that was a Plymouth. I never owned a goddamn Studebaker.

EDDIE: This went on for years. He kept disappearing and reappearing. For years that went on. Then, suddenly one day it stopped. He stayed home for a while. Just stayed in the house. Never went outside. Just sat in his chair. Staring. Then he started going on these long walks. He'd walk all day. Then he'd walk all night. He'd walk out across the fields. In the dark. I used to watch him from my bedroom window. He'd disappear in the dark with his overcoat on.

MARTIN: Where was he going?

EDDIE: Just walking.

THE OLD MAN: I was making a decision.

(Eddie gets Martin to his feet and takes him on a walk around the entire stage as he tells the story. Martin is reluctant but Eddie keeps pulling him along.)

EDDIE: But one night I asked him if I could go with him. And he took me. We walked straight out across the fields together. In the dark.

And I remember it was just plowed and our feet sank down in the powder and the dirt came up over the tops of my shoes and weighted me down. I wanted to stop and empty my shoes out but he wouldn't stop. He kept walking straight ahead and I was afraid of losing him in the dark so I just kept up as best I could. And we were completely silent the whole time. Never said a word to each other. We could barely see a foot in front of us, it was so dark. And these white owls kept swooping down out of nowhere, hunting for jackrabbits. Diving right past our heads, then disappearing. And we just kept walking silent like that for miles until we got to town. I could see the drive-in movie way off in the distance. That was the first thing I saw. Just square patches of color shifting. Then vague faces began to appear. And, as we got closer, I could recognize one of the faces. It was Spencer Tracy. Spencer Tracy moving his mouth. Speaking without words. Speaking to a woman in a red dress. Then we stopped at a liquor store and he made me wait outside in the parking lot while he bought a bottle. And there were all these Mexican migrant workers standing around a pickup truck with red mud all over their tires. They were drinking beer and laughing and I remember being jealous of them and I didn't know why. And I remember seeing the old man through the glass door of the liquor store as he paid for the bottle. I remember feeling sorry for him and I didn't know why. Then he came outside with the bottle wrapped in a brown paper sack and as soon as he came out, all the Mexican men stopped laughing. They just stared at us as we walked away.

(During the course of the story the lights shift down very slowly into blues and greens — moonlight.)

EDDIE: And we walked right through town. Past the donut shop, past the miniature golf course, past the Chevron station. And he opened the bottle up and offered it to me. Before he even took a drink, he offered it to me first. And I took it and drank it and handed it back to him. And we just kept passing it back and forth like that as we walked until we drank the whole thing dry. And we never said a word the whole time. Then, finally we reached this little white house with a red awning, on the far side of town. I'll never forget the red awning because it slapped in the night breeze and the porch light made it glow. It was a hot, desert breeze and the air smelled like new-cut alfalfa. We walked right up to the front porch and he rang the bell and I remember getting real nervous because I wasn't expecting to visit anybody. I thought we were just out for a walk. And then this woman comes to the door. This real pretty woman with red hair. And she throws herself into his arms. And he starts crying. He just breaks down right there in front of me. And she's kissing him all over the face and holding him real tight and he's just crying like a baby. And then through the doorway, behind them both, I see this girl.

(The bathroom door very slowly and silently swings open revealing May, standing in the doorframe backlit with yellow light in her red dress. She just watches Eddie as he keeps telling the story. He and Martin are unaware of her presence.)

EDDIE: She just appears. She's just standing there, staring at me and I'm staring back at her and we can't take our eyes off each other. It was like we knew each other from somewhere but we couldn't place where. But the second we saw each other, that very second, we knew we'd never stop being in love.

(May slams bathroom door behind. Door booms. Lights bang back up to their previous setting.)

MAY: *(To Eddie.)* Boy, you really are incredible! You're unbelievable! Martin comes over here. He doesn't know you from Adam and you start telling him a story like that. Are you crazy? None of it's true, Martin. He's had this weird, sick idea for years now and it's totally made up. He's nuts. I don't know where he got it from. He's completely nuts.

EDDIE: *(To Martin.)* She's kinda' embarrassed about the whole deal, see. You can't blame her really.

MARTIN: I didn't even know you could hear us out here, May. I —
MAY: I heard every word. I followed it very carefully. He's told me that story a thousand times and it always changes.
EDDIE: I never repeat myself.
MAY: You do nothing but repeat yourself. That's all you do. You just go in a big circle.
MARTIN: *(Standing.)* Well, maybe I should leave.
EDDIE: NO! You sit down.

(Silence. Martin slowly sits again.)

EDDIE: *(Quietly to Martin, leaning toward him.)* Did you think that was a story, Martin? Did you think I made that whole thing up?
MARTIN: No. I mean, at the time you were telling it, it seemed real.
EDDIE: But now you're doubting it because she says it's a lie?
MARTIN: Well —
EDDIE: She suggests it's a lie to you and all of a sudden you change your mind? Is that it? You go from true to false like that, in a second?
MARTIN: I don't know.
MAY: Let's go to the movies, Martin.

(Martin stands again.)

EDDIE: Sit down!

(Martin sits back down. Long pause.)

MAY: Eddie —

(Pause.)

EDDIE: What?
MAY: We want to go to the movies.

(Pause. Eddie just stares at her.)

MAY: I want to go out to the movies with Martin. Right now.

EDDIE: Nobody's going to the movies. There's not a movie in this town that can match the story I'm gonna' tell. I'm gonna' finish this story.
MAY: Eddie —
EDDIE: You wanna' hear the rest of the story, don't ya', Martin?
MARTIN: *(Pause. He looks at May, then back to Eddie.)* Sure.
MAY: Martin, let's go. Please.
MARTIN: I —

(Long pause. Eddie and Martin stare at each other.)

EDDIE: You what?
MARTIN: I don't mind hearing the rest of it if you want to tell the rest of it.
THE OLD MAN: *(To himself.)* I'm dyin' to hear it myself.

(Eddie leans back in his chair. Grins.)

MAY: *(To Eddie.)* What do you think this is going to do? Do you think this is going to change something?
EDDIE: No.
MAY: Then what's the point?
EDDIE: It's absolutely pointless.
MAY: Then why put everybody through this. Martin doesn't want to hear this bullshit. *I* don't want to hear it.
EDDIE: I know *you* don't wanna' hear it.
MAY: Don't try to pass it off on me! You got it all turned around, Eddie. You got it all turned around. You don't even know which end is up anymore. Okay. Okay. I don't need either of you. I don't need any of it because I already know the rest of the story. I know the whole rest of the story , see. *(She speaks directly to Eddie, who remains sitting.)* I know it just exactly the way it happened. Without any little tricks added to it.

(The Old Man leans over to Eddie, confidentially.)

THE OLD MAN: What does she know?

EDDIE: *(To The Old Man.)* She's lying.

(Lights begin to shift down again in the course of May's story. She moves very slowly downstage, then crosses toward The Old Man as she tells it.)

MAY: You want me to finish the story for you, Eddie? Huh? You want me to finish this story?

(Pause as Martin sits again.)

MAY: See, my mother — the pretty red-haired woman in the little white house with the red awning — was desperately in love with the old man. Wasn't she, Eddie? You could tell that right away. You could see it in her eyes. She was obsessed with him to the point where she couldn't stand being without him for even a second. She kept hunting for him from town to town. Following little clues that he left behind, like a postcard maybe, or a motel on the back of a matchbook. *(To Martin.)* He never left her a phone number or an address or anything as simple as that because my mother was his secret, see. She hounded him for years and he kept trying to keep her at a distance because the closer these two separate lives drew together, these two separate women, these two separate kids, the more nervous he got. The more filled with terror that the two lives would find out about each other and devour him whole. That his secret would take him by the throat. But finally she caught up with him. Just by a process of elimination she dogged him down. I remember the day we discovered the town. She was on fire. "This is it!" she kept saying; "this is the place!" Her whole body was trembling as we walked through the streets, looking for the house where he lived. She kept squeezing my hand to the point where I thought she'd crush the bones in my fingers. She was terrified she'd come across him by accident on the street because she knew she was trespassing. She knew she was crossing this forbidden zone but she couldn't help herself. We walked all day through that stupid hick town. All day long. We went through every neighborhood, peering through every open window, looking in at every dumb family, until finally we found him.

(Rest.)

It was just exactly suppertime and they were all sitting down at the table and they were having fried chicken. That's how close we were to the window. We could see what they were eating. We could hear their voices but we couldn't make out what they were saying. Eddie and his mother were talking but the old man never said a word. Did he, Eddie? Just sat there eating his chicken in silence.

THE OLD MAN: *(To Eddie.)* Boy, is she ever off the wall with this one. You gotta' do somethin' about this.

MAY: The funny thing was, that almost as soon as we'd found him — he disappeared. She was only with him about two weeks before he just vanished. Nobody saw him after that. Ever. And my mother — just turned herself inside out. I never could understand that. I kept watching her grieve, as though somebody'd died. She'd pull herself up into a ball and just stare at the floor. And I couldn't understand that because I was feeling the exact opposite feeling. I was in love, see. I'd come home after school, after being with Eddie, and I was filled with this joy and there she'd be — standing in the middle of the kitchen staring at the sink. Her eyes looked like a funeral. And I didn't know what to say. I didn't even feel sorry for her. All I could think of was him.

THE OLD MAN: *(To Eddie.)* She's gettin' way outa' line, here.

MAY: And all he could think of was me. Isn't that right, Eddie. We couldn't take a breath without thinking of each other. We couldn't eat if we weren't together. We couldn't sleep. We got sick at night when we were apart. Violently sick. And my mother even took me to see a doctor. And Eddie's mother took him to see the same doctor but the doctor had no idea what was wrong with ut. He thought it was the flu or something. And Eddie's mother had no idea what was wrong with him. But my mother — my mother knew exactly what was wrong.

She knew it clear down to her bones. She recognized every symptom. And she begged me not to see him but I wouldn't listen. Then she begged Eddie not to see me but he wouldn't listen. Then she went to Eddie's mother and begged her. And Eddie's mother — *(Pause. She looks straight at Eddie.)* — Eddie's mother blew her brains out. Didn't she, Eddie? Blew her brains right out.

THE OLD MAN: *(Standing. He moves from the platform onto the stage, between Eddie and May.)* Now, wait a second! Wait a second. Just a goddamn second here. This story doesn't hold water. *(To Eddie, who stays seated.)* You're not gonna let her off the hook with that one are ya? That's the dumbest version I ever heard in my whole life. She never blew her brains out. Nobody ever told me that. Where the hell did that come from? *(To Eddie, who remains seated.)* Stand up! Get on yer feet now goddammit! I wanna' hear the male side a' this thing. You gotta represent me now. Speak on my behalf. There's no one to speak for me now? Stand up!

(Eddie stands slowly. Stares at The Old Man.)

THE OLD MAN: Now tell her. Tell her the way it happened. We've got a pact. Don't forget that.

EDDIE: *(Calmly to The Old Man.)* It was your shotgun. Same one we used to duck-hunt with. Browning. She never fired a gun before in her life. That was her first time.

THE OLD MAN: Nobody told me any a' that. I was left completely in the dark.

EDDIE: You were gone.

THE OLD MAN: Somebody could've found me! Somebody could've hunted me down. I wasn't that impossible to find.

EDDIE: You were gone.

****

THE READING ROOM

YOUNG ACTORS AND THEIR TEACHERS

DeRose, David J. *Sam Shepard.* New York: Maxwell Macmillan International, 1992.

Graham, Laura J. "Sam Shepard," in *Dictionary of Literary Biography, Vol. 341: Twentieth-Century American Dramatists, Fifth Series.* Edited by Garrett Eisler. Columbia, S.C.:Bruccoli Clark Layman Book, 2008.

Wilcox, Leonard, ed. *Rereading Shepard: Contemporary Critical Essays on the Plays of Sam Shepard.* New York: St. Martin's Press, 1993.

SCHOLARS, STUDENTS, PROFESSORS

Callens, Johan, ed. *Contemporary Theatre Review: An International Journal: Sam Shepard: Between the Margin and the Centre (1).* Vol. 8, Part 3. Newark, N.J.: Gordon & Breach Publishing Group, 1998.

__________. *Contemporary Theatre Review: An International Journal. Sam Shepard: Between the Margin and the Center (2).* Vol. 8, Part 4. Newark, N.J.: Gordon & Breach Publishing Group, 1998.

Chubb, Kenneth et al. "Metaphors, Mad Dogs and Old-Time Cowboys," *Theatre Quarterly.* Vol. IV, No. 15. (August–October 1974) 3–16. Reprinted in *American Dreams: The Imagination of Sam Shepard,* edited by Bonnie Marranca. New York: Performing Arts Journal Publications, 1981, pp. 187–209.

Hart, Lynda. *Sam Shepard's Metaphorical Stages.* Westport, Conn.: Greenwood Press, 1987.

King, Kimball. *Ten Modern American Playwrights: An Annotated Bibliography.* New York: Garland Publishers, 1982.

__________. *Sam Shepard: A Casebook.* New York: Garland Publishers, 1988.

Kolin, Philip C. *American Playwrights Since 1945: A Guide to Scholarship, Criticism, and Performance.* New York: Greenwood Press, 1989.

This extensive bibliography lists books about the playwright according to whom the books might be of interest. If you would like to research further something that interests you in the text, lists of references, sources cited, and editions used in this book are found in this section.

Kroll, Jack, Constance Guthrie, and Janet Huck. "Who's That Tall, Dark Stranger?" *Newsweek* (November 11, 1985): 71.

McGhee, Jim. *True Lies: The Architecture of the Fantastic in the Plays of Sam Shepard.* New York: Peter Lang Publishing, 1993.

Mottram, Ron. *Inner Landscapes: The Theater of Sam Shepard.* Columbia: University of Missouri Press, 1976.

"Sam Shepard: Stalking Himself," *Great Performances,* PBS, July 8, 1998.

Shepard, Sam. *Rolling Thunder Logbook.* New York: Viking Press, 1977.

Tucker, Martin. *Sam Shepard.* New York: Continuum, 1992.

Wade, Leslie A. *Sam Shepard and the American Theatre.* Westport, Conn.: Greenwood Press, 1997.

THEATERS, PRODUCERS

Auerbach, Doris. *Sam Shepard, Arthur Kopit, and the Off Broadway Theater.* Boston: Twayne Publishers, 1982.

Daniels, Barry, ed. *Joseph Chaikin & Sam Shepard: Letters and Texts, 1972–1984.* New York: New American Library, 1989.

Marranca, Bonnie, ed. *American Dreams: The Imagination of Sam Shepard.* New York: Performing Arts Journal Publications, 1981.

ACTORS, DIRECTORS, THEATER PROFESSIONALS

Bottoms, Stephen J. *The Theatre of Sam Shepard: States of Crisis.* New York: Cambridge University Press, 1998.

Graham, Laura J. *Sam Shepard: Theme, Image and the Director.* New York: Peter Lang Publishing, 1995.

Mailman, Bruce and Poland, Albert. *The Off-Off Broadway Book.* New York: Bobbs-Merrill,1972.

Rosen, Carol. "Silent Tongues: Sam Shepard's Explorations of Emotional Territory," *The Village Voice* (August 4, 1992): 32–41.

THE EDITIONS OF SHEPARD'S WORKS USED FOR THIS BOOK

Shepard, Sam. *The Mad Dog Blues & Other Plays: Cowboy Mouth, The Rock Garden, Cowboy's #2.* New York: Winter House, 1972.

___________. *Curse of the Starving Class: A Play in Three Acts.* New York: Dramatists Play Service, 1976.

___________. *Angel City & Other Plays: Curse of the Starving Class, Killer's Head, Action, The Mad Dog Blues, Cowboy Mouth, The Rock*

Garden, Cowboy's #2; Patti Smith's "9 Random Years (7&2)." New York: Urizen Books, 1976.
__________. *Buried Child.* New York: Urizen Books, 1978.
__________. *Buried Child & Seduced & Suicide in B Flat.* New York: Urizen Books, 1979.
__________. *True West.* Garden City, N.Y.: Nelson Doubleday, 1981.
__________. *Sam Shepard: Seven Plays: Buried Child, Curse of the Starving Class, The Tooth of Crime, La Turista, Tongues, Savage Love, True West.* New York: Bantam Books, 1981.
__________. *Fool For Love and The Sad Lament of Pecos Bill on the Eve of Killing His Wife.* San Francisco: City Lights Books, 1983.
__________. *Fool For Love & Other Plays: Angel City, Melodrama Play, Cowboy Mouth, Action, Suicide in B Flat, Seduced, Geography of a Horse Dreamer.* New York: Bantam Books, 1984.
__________. *Fool For Love & Other Plays: Angel City, Melodrama Play, Cowboy Mouth, Action, Suicide in B Flat, Seduced, Geography of a Horse Dreamer.* New York: Bantam Books, 1984.

SOURCES CITED IN THIS BOOK

Oumano, Ellen. *Sam Shepard: The Life and Work of an American Dreamer.* New York: St. Martin's Press, 1986.
Sessums, Kevin. "Sam Shepard: Geography of a Horse Dreamer," *Interview* (1988): 71
Senior, Jennifer. "Sam Shepard," *New York* (February 9, 1998): 45.
Shewey, Don. *Sam Shepard: The Life, the Loves Behind the Legend of a True American.* New York: Dell Publishing, 1985.
__________. *Sam Shepard.* New York: Da Capo Press, 1997.

"And the winner is . . ."

	PULITZER PRIZE	TONY AWARD	NY DRAMA CRITICS CIRCLE AWARD Best American	Best Foreign	Best Play
1964	No Award	John Osborne *Luther*	John Osborne *Luther*		
1965	Frank D. Gilroy *The Subject Was Roses*	Frank D. Gilroy *The Subject Was Roses*	Frank D. Gilroy *The Subject Was Roses*		
1966	No Award	Peter Weiss *Marat / Sade*	Peter Weiss *Marat / Sade*		
1967	Edward Albee *A Delicate Balance*	Harold Pinter *The Homecoming*	Harold Pinter *The Homecoming*		
1968	No Award	Tom Stoppard *Rosencrantz and Guildenstern Are Dead*	Tom Stoppard *Rosencrantz and Guildenstern Are Dead*		
1969	Howard Sackler *The Great White Hope*	Howard Sackler *The Great White Hope*	Howard Sackler *The Great White Hope*		
1970	Charles Gordone *No Place to Be Somebody*	Frank McMahon *Borstal Boy*	Paul Zindel *The Effect of Gamma Rays on Man-in-the-Moon Marigolds*	No Award	Frank McMahon *Borstal Boy*
1971	Paul Zindel *The Effect of Gamma Rays on Man-in-the-Moon Marigolds*	Anthony Shaffer *Sleuth*	John Guare *The House of Blue Leaves*	No Award	David Storey *Home*
1972	No Award	David Rabe *Sticks and Bones*	No Award	Jean Genet *The Screens*	Jason Miller *That Championship Season*
1973	Jason Miller *That Championship Season*	Jason Miller *That Champion Season*	Lanford Wilson *The Hot L Baltimore*	No Award	David Storey *The Changing Room*
1974	No Award	Joseph A. Walker *The River Niger*	Miguel Pinero *Short Eyes*	No Award	David Storey *The Contractor*

	PULITZER PRIZE	TONY AWARD	NY DRAMA CRITICS CIRCLE AWARD		
			Best American	Best Foreign	Best Play
1975	Edward Albee *Seascape*	Peter Shaffer *Equus*	Ed Bullins *The Taking of Miss Janie*	No Award	Peter Shaffer *Equus*
1976	Marvin Hamlisch, music Edward Kleban, lyrics Nicholas Dante, book James Kirkwood, book *A Chorus Line*	Tom Stoppard *Travesties*	David Rabe *Streamers*	No Award	Tom Stoppard *Travesties*
1977	Michael Cristofer *The Shadow Box*	Michael Cristofer *The Shadow Box*	David Mamet *American Buffalo*	No Award	Simon Gray *Otherwise Engaged*
1978	Donald L. Coburn *The Gin Game*	Hugh Leonard *Da*	Hugh Leonard *Da*		
1979	**Sam Shepard** ***Buried Child***	Bernard Pomerance *The Elephant Man*	Bernard Pomerance *The Elephant Man*		
1980	Lanford Wilson *Talley's Folly*	Mark Medoff *Children of a Lesser God*	No Award	Harold Pinter *Betrayal*	Lanford Wilson *Talley's Folly*
1981	Beth Henley *Crimes of the Heart*	Peter Shaffer *Amadeus*	Beth Henley *Crimes of the Heart*	No Award	Athol Fugard *A Lesson from Aloes*
1982	Charles Fuller *A Soldier's Play*	David Edgar *The Life and Adventures of Nicholas Nickleby*	Charles Fuller *A Soldier's Play*	No Award	David Edgar *The Life and Adventures of Nicholas Nickleby*
1983	Marsha Norman *Night, Mother*	Harvey Fierstein *Torch Song Trilogy*	No Award	David Hare *Plenty*	Neil Simon *Brighton Beach Memoirs*
1984	David Mamet *Glengarry Glen Ross*	Tom Stoppard *The Real Thing*	David Mamet *Glengarry Glen Ross*	No Award	Tom Stoppard *The Real Thing*
1985	Stephen Sondheim, music/lyrics James Lapine, book *Sunday in the Park with George*	Neil Simon *Biloxi Blues*	August Wilson *Ma Rainey's Black Bottom*		
1986	No Award	Herb Gardener *I'm Not Rappaport*	Michael Frayn *Benefactors*	No Award	**Sam Shepard** ***A Lie of the Mind***
1987	August Wilson *Fences*	August Wilson *Fences*	No Award	Christopher Hampton *Les Liaisons Dangereuses*	August Wilson *Fences*

	PULITZER PRIZE	TONY AWARD	NY DRAMA CRITICS CIRCLE AWARD		
			Best American	Best Foreign	Best Play
1988	Alfred Uhry *Driving Miss Daisy*	David Henry Hwang *M. Butterfly*	No Award	Athol Fugard *Road to Mecca*	August Wilson *Joe Turner's Come and Gone*
1989	Wendy Wasserstein *The Heidi Chronicles*	Wendy Wasserstein *The Heidi Chronicles*	No Award	Brian Friel *Aristocrats*	Wendy Wasserstein *The Heidi Chronicles*
1990	August Wilson *The Piano Lesson*	Frank Galati *The Grapes of Wrath*	No Award	Peter Nichols *Privates on Parade*	August Wilson *The Piano Lesson*
1991	Neil Simon *Lost in Yonkers*	Neil Simon *Lost in Yonkers*	No Award	Timberlake Wertenbaker *Our Country's Good*	John Guare *Six Degrees of Separation*
1992	Robert Schenkkan *The Kentucky Cycle*	Brian Friel *Dancing at Lughnasa*	August Wilson *Two Trains Running*	No Award	Brian Friel *Dancing at Lughnasa*
1993	Tony Kushner *Angels in America: Millennium Approaches*	Tony Kushner *Angels in America: Millennium Approaches*	No Award	Frank McGuinness *Someone Who'll Watch Over Me*	Tony Kushner *Angels in America: Millennium Approaches*
1994	Edward Albee *Three Tall Women*	Tony Kushner *Angels in America: Perestroika*	Edward Albee *Three Tall Women*		
1995	Horton Foote *The Young Man From Atlanta*	Terrence McNally *Love! Valour! Compassion!*	Terrence McNally *Love! Valour! Compassion!*	No Award	Tom Stoppard *Arcadia*
1996	Jonathan Larson *Rent*	Terrence McNally *Master Class*	No Award	Brian Friel *Molly Sweeney*	August Wilson *Seven Guitars*
1997	No Award	Alfred Uhry *The Last Night of Ballyhoo*	No Award	David Hare *Skylight*	Paula Vogel *How I Learned to Drive*
1998	Paula Vogel *How I Learned to Drive*	Yasmina Reza *Art*	Tina Howe *Pride's Crossing*	No Award	Yasmina Reza *Art*
1999	Margaret Edson *Wit*	Warren Leight *Side Man*	No Award	Patrick Marber *Closer*	Margaret Edson *Wit*

	PULITZER PRIZE	TONY AWARD	NY DRAMA CRITICS CIRCLE AWARD		
			Best American	Best Foreign	Best Play
2000	Donald Margulies *Dinner with Friends*	Michael Frayn *Copenhagen*	No Award	Michael Frayn *Copenhagen*	August Wilson *Jitney*
2001	David Auburn *Proof*	David Auburn *Proof*	David Auburn *Proof*	No Award	Tom Stoppard *The Invention of Love*
2002	Suzan-Lori Parks *Topdog/Underdog*	Edward Albee *The Goat: or, Who Is Sylvia?*	Edward Albee *The Goat: or, Who Is Sylvia?*		
2003	Nilo Cruz *Anna in the Tropics*	Richard Greenburg *Take Me Out*	No Award	Alan Bennett *Talking Heads*	Richard Greenburg *Take Me Out*
2004	Doug Wright *I Am My Own Wife*	Doug Wright *I Am My Own Wife*	Lynn Nottage *Intimate Apparel*		
2005	John Patrick Shanley *Doubt, a Parable*	John Patrick Shanley *Doubt, a Parable*	No Award	Martin McDonagh *The Pillowman*	John Patrick Shanley *Doubt, a Parable*
2006	No Award	Alan Bennet *The History Boys*	Alan Bennett *The History Boys*		
2007	David Lindsay-Abaire *Rabbit Hole*	Tom Stoppard *The Coast of Utopia*	August Wilson *Radio Gulf*	No Award	Tom Stoppard *The Coast of Utopia*
2008	Tracy Letts *August: Osage County*	Tracy Letts *August: Osage County*	Tracy Letts *August: Osage County*		

INDEX

The entries in the index include highlights from the main In an Hour essay portion of the book.

ABOUT THE AUTHOR

Laura J. Graham received her M.A. in English literature and Ph.D. in theater arts from the University of California at Los Angeles. Her specializations include critical studies in modern and contemporary British and American drama, directing, and studies in performance theory. An alumna of the Lee Strasberg Theatre Institute, she has taught acting and directing and served as the producing director of the four theaters that comprise the Lee Strasberg Creative Center in Los Angeles. Graham has produced and directed many works by Sam Shepard, including *Tongues*, *Savage Love* (written in collaboration with Joseph Chaikin), *Fool for Love*, and *Buried Child*, which garnered *Drama-Log* awards for best performance and direction. She has served as guest lecturer in directing at UCLA; adjunct faculty at Antioch University, Los Angeles, and Marymount Manhattan College; and as the theater program director at the College of Staten Island/CUNY. Graham is the author of numerous articles, including the entry on Sam Shepard in the recently published *Dictionary of Literary Biography, Vol. 341: Twentieth-Century American Dramatists, Fifth Series* and the book, *Sam Shepard: Theme, Image & the Director*. She served as the scholar/lecturer for the 1988 Taper Playviews at the Mark Taper Forum, Los Angeles, where she presented a paper on Shepard's relationship to and breaks with dramatic and theatrical tradition, relationship to elements of Romanticism, and his use and manipulation of American mythos and led a post-performance cast/audience discussion of Sam Shepard's *Lie of the Mind*. Graham is currently pursuing research and writing projects as an independent scholar.

NOTE FROM THE PUBLISHER

We thank Bantam Books, a division of Random House, whose enlightened permissions policy reflects an understanding that copyright law is intended to both protect the rights of creators of intellectual property as well as to encourage its use for the public good.